NEW ZEALAND
Portrait of a Nation

Brian McClintock collection

New Zealand Memories

Graham Stewart

Streams and rivers were slowly conquered, allowing travellers to proceed in comfort around New Zealand. First it was river pontoon ferries; then upper-truss wooden bridges tied together with a lattice of steel rods were built, later to be replaced with steel and concrete structures.

New Zealand is 1,600 km long and 450 km wide at its widest part. Covering an area of approximately 270,500 sq km, all islands combined. It is about the size of the United Kingdom or Japan.

Following page (from top left): The flagpole at Waitangi; The Strand, Russell; The container ship *Maersk Duffield* enters the Waitemata Harbour; Mt Taranaki; Grape vines, Upper Moutere, Nelson; Danseys Pass Coach Inn (built 1862); Queenstown on Lake Wakatipu; Signpost at Bluff.

All photographs Graham Stewart

Yesterday and Today

NEW ZEALAND
Portrait of a Nation

GRAHAM STEWART

Published with the grateful assistance of the following sponsors

kiwi bank It's ours
www.kiwibank.co.nz

KiwiRail
www.kiwirail.co.nz

NewstalkZB®
www.newstalkzb.co.nz

Sunday Star Times
www.sstlive.co.nz

THE
DOMINION POST
www.dompost.co.nz

Waikato Times
As Waikato As It Gets
www.waikatotimes.co.nz

TARANAKI
DAILY NEWS
Your Place, Your Paper
www.taranakidailynews.co.nz

Manawatu
Standard
www.manawatustandard.co.nz

THE PRESS
www.press.co.nz

The Southland Times
www.southlandtimes.co.nz

BDT
www.bdt.co.nz

PocockHudson
www.pocockhudson.co.nz

SPY VALLEY
www.spyvalleywine.co.nz

ARA
www.winegrowersofara.co.nz

EUROWINE

For New Zealand and for my daughters
Anna Pocock and Jane Woodrow

Graham Ste...

Contents

Maps	8, 9
Introduction	10
The North Island	17
Northland	19
Auckland	49
Coromandel Peninsula – Thames	69
Waikato and the Hauraki Plains	73
The King Country	81
Rotorua and the Bay of Plenty	85
Eastland	95
Gisborne	104
Taupo and the Volcanic Plateau	109
Rangitikei, Manawatu and Wanganui	119
Taranaki	131
Hawke's Bay	143
The Wairarapa	161
Wellington Region – the Hutt Valley	171

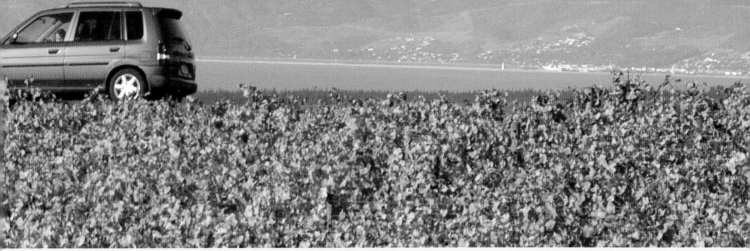

Grape vines in the Nelson district. *all photographs Graham Stewart*

The South Island 189

Marlborough and Nelson Region 191

The West Coast 205

North Canterbury 229

Christchurch 233

Central and South Canterbury 249

Otago 263

Dunedin 267

Otago 280

Central Otago 285

Queenstown and Lakes District 295

Fiordland 305

Southland 311

Stewart Island 319

Author Postscript 321

Acknowledgements 322

Index 325

Cape Reinga

Houhora

Whangaroa

Waitangi

Mangonui

Kaitaia

Kerikeri

Otehei Bay
Cape Brett

North Waimate

Paihia

Russell

Kohukohu

Opua

Rawene

Kaikohe

Kawakawa

Opononi

Ohaeawai

Waipoua Forest

WHANGAREI

Dargaville

Waipu

Matakohe

Wellsford

Warkworth

Puhoi

Waiwera

Helensville

Orewa

Waiheke Island

Coromandel

Whitianga

AUCKLAND

Pukekohe

Thames

Mercer

Paeroa

Waihi

Te Aroha

Ngaruawahia

Morrinsville

Mount Maunganui

Ruakokore

Hicks Bay

HAMILTON

TAURANGA

Te Kaha

Te Araroa

Raglan

Matamata

Te Puke

Tikitiki

Te Awamutu

Cambridge

Whakatane

Opotiki

Ruatoria

Waitomo

Otorohanga

ROTORUA

Tokomaru Bay

Te Kuiti

Tolaga Bay

Wairakei

Taupo

Lake Waikaremoana

GISBORNE

Taumarunui

Rangitaiki

NEW PLYMOUTH

Whangamomona

Raurimu

Mount Tongariro

Wairoa

Mount Ngauruhoe

Tarawera

Mount Taranaki

Stratford

Chateau

Mount Ruapehu

Mohaka

Opunake

Eltham

Ohakune

Waiouru

Hawera

Tangiwai

NAPIER

Taihape

HASTINGS

Havelock North

Mangaweka

WANGANUI

Hunterville

Waipawa

Marton

Waipukurau

Bulls

Feilding

Dannevirke

PALMERSTON NORTH

Woodville

Taumata....

Pahiatua

Levin

Eketahuna

MASTERTON

Paekakariki

Carterton

Featherston

Greytown

LOWER HUTT

Martinborough

WELLINGTON

Rimutakas

Bainham • • Collingwood
• Takaka

Karamea • Motueka • • NELSON Havelock
Wakefield • • Brightwater • Picton
• Blenheim

Denniston • • Glenhope
Westport • • Murchison
Charleston • *Hawks Crag*
Punakaiki • • Reefton *Parititahi Tunnels*

Greymouth • • Blackball • Kaikoura
Taramakau • Hanmer Springs *Raramai Tunnels*
Hokitika • Otira •
Ross • • Arthur's Pass
• Cass

Franz Joseph Glacier Rangiora
Fox Glacier • Kaiapoi
Mount Cook • CHRISTCHURCH
Lyttelton
• Akaroa

Lake Tekapo • Ashburton
Haast •
• Fairlie
• Waitohi
• TIMARU

Milford Sound
Skippers Canyon • Wanaka • Waimate
• Cardrona • Danseys Pass
Arrowtown St. Bathans •
Homer Tunnel Wedderburn • Oamaru
Queenstown • Cromwell • Poolburn
Doubtful Sound Clyde • Alexandra
Moeraki Boulders
• Kingston
• Te Anau

Wilmot Pass
• Port Chalmers
Heriot • Wingatui • DUNEDIN

Gore • Clinton
Winton • • Mataura Kaitangata
Riverton • Balclutha
INVERCARGILL •
Bluff •

STEWART ISLAND
Oban
Halfmoon Bay

Graham Stewart

Before motorised machinery – a threshing mill team at work near Havelock North in the late 1950s. The large flywheel of the traction engine drives the belts which take power to the mill. Men bag the grain at one end of the mill and at the other a lift, also powered by the traction engine, carries the straw to the top of the stack.

Introduction

This book takes you on an historical journey back in time from Cape Reinga in the north to Halfmoon Bay on Stewart Island. In the North Island alone, there are 375 provincial cities and towns, in the South Island 234, a total of over 600, so those featured in the book are a selection only.

The majority of the historic photographs have been matched with photographs taken in the same position today, to make it easy for the reader to identify the locations. The photographs show the vast changes in our style of living over the years: the pioneer unsealed muddy roads, past and present bridge structures, transportation by road, rail and sea, agriculture, sport and tourism. They depict the good times and the tragedies. This book also features New Zealanders who have made the country what it is today; others who broke the mould and were the first to achieve in their chosen careers.

New Zealand was at the end of the world, in the Antipodes, when it became an outpost of the British Empire in 1840. European settlement brought with it architecture from the northern hemisphere which

Mr J.B. McNaughton ploughing with a six-horse team at Glen Murray in November 1956.

was adapted to suit the climate and our style of living. Timber was plentiful and used in preference to other materials in the 19th century and the early years of the 20th century. Over time fire destroyed many classic Victorian and Edwardian buildings; then the lack of appreciation for heritage buildings meant many fell victim to the demolition hammer. In more recent years the work of the New Zealand Historic Places Trust has educated the populace to the value of our architectural heritage, and many imposing structures have now been saved and restored.

This book shows some of the survivors; other scenes of our towns and cities show unbelievable change where there is, sadly, not a trace of the original roads or buildings.

This is not a book of pretty sunset and sunrise photographs. It illustrates the change to our country over the decades and gives an insight into New Zealand's past that our children and grandchildren should study in order to appreciate what has gone before and be aware of our heritage.

Before the automobile – when horsepower had real legs

A.N. Breckon, Graham Stewart collection

The cabbies' stand in Victoria Street East, Auckland, c1909, with the old Central Hotel in the background.

In the 1900s an Auckland cab driver gives his two-horsepower vehicle a drink at a horse trough in Victoria Street East, Auckland, opposite where Whitcoulls is today on the corner of Queen Street.

A.N. Breckon, Graham Stewart collection

Like the motorcar of today – there was a selection of horse-drawn carriage styles to choose from. This showroom was at Stratford, Taranaki.

The high-wheeled perambulators of the 19th century returned to fashion briefly in the latter years of the 20th century before the advent of the buggies of today.

New Zealand has always had a love affair with the automobile

Mr and Mrs P.R. Skeates of Auckland in the Manawatu Gorge during their honeymoon in 1905. The car was a 12 h.p. Darracq.

The early motorist had to carry a full emergency kit and be prepared for any drama ahead.

All photographs Graham Stewart collection

Above: A Parliamentary tour of Northland in 1917 struck a problem between Herekino and Kohukohu.

Right and below: Four-wheel-drive vehicles have made exploring the back country a popular and exhilarating experience.

Graham Stewart

Graham Stewart

The first woman conductor was a Miss W. Mitchell on Searle's motorbus at Oamaru in 1916.

The first A.A. signs truck used for road signposting in Auckland Province, seen in 1929 on the highway between Helensville and Port Albert.

Cars and caravans in convoy in the early days of the Cambridge Caravan Club.

all photographs Graham Stewart collection

The Maori haka bonds the nation: a challenge to visitors and sports teams

A Ngati Tuwharetoa group performing the haka at the Waitangi celebrations in 1934. As historian Michael King wrote, 'The leap signifies the climax of the dance. The Haka was never simply a war dance, although it is frequently described as such. It was a posture dance that served several functions. In earlier years it kept warriors physically and psychologically toned up for battle in much the same way as military drill. But it was and is also a ritual of assertion and defiance. It establishes and flaunts masculinity, and the identity of the group performing it.' It has become a feature of ceremonies to welcome visitors on to marae. Today it is a tradition for the All Blacks to perform the haka at the start of international rugby test matches.

Below: An icon in the world of rugby photography, Peter Bush, captured the All Blacks in haka action at the test match at Hamilton Stadium against Canada in June 2007.

The North Island

Total area: 113729 km²
Maori name: Te Ika a Maui
(the fish of Maui)

The first motor trip between Wellington and Auckland in 1912 went through Taihape, Taumarunui and Te Kuiti over clay and dirt roads. In the foreground a dog chases after the model T Ford motorcar that made the first historic journey.

The humble cow has been vital to our world trade in dairy products

European settlers brought cows to our shores, and as the land was cleared and pastures sown, milking sheds and holding yards were built of basic timber materials. The first cooperative dairy company was established in 1871 at Springfield on the Otago Peninsula. Milking the herds by hand was slowly replaced by machines; by 1918 about half the cows were being milked by machines. Circular automated milking halls of the 21st century are designed so farmers can place the milking cups on the cows at eye level from a pit below, so ending the back-bending task.

Northland

The Te Waimate Mission House at Waimate North, just north of Ohaeawai where Charles Darwin and early pioneers stayed, was the site of New Zealand's first European farm. It is the only survivor of three mission houses built in 1831-1832 by Maori carpenters with local materials. Bishop Selwyn lived here for two years before moving to Auckland.

The core of Pompallier House on the Strand at Russell was built by a process known as pisé de terre (rammed earth) to accommodate the Roman Catholic Mission's printing press in 1841-1842. The building was the headquarters of the Marist Mission to Oceania (1801-1871), and although Bishop Pompallier never lived here, the house was named after him by a resident in 1913.

Tiki postcard – Pictorial Publication Limited, Hastings, c1970s. William Main collection

CAPE REINGA LIGHTHOUSE, NORTHLAND, N.Z.

Graham Stewart

Latitude 34° 25.7' South
Longitude 172° 40.6 East

At the end of the road along the narrow Aupouri Peninsula, 116 km from Kaitaia, is Cape Reinga (Te Rerenga Wairoa), the symbolic furthest point north. Surville Cliffs to the east is closer to the equator by 4.8 kilometres. The lighthouse, which first shone in May 1941, stands guardian over the meeting of the mighty oceans. The original lighthouse built in 1879 was on Motuopaoi Island, out from Cape Maria van Diemen. The Cape Reinga lighthouse, built during the Second World War, was fully automated in 1987 and is now managed by a computer and maritime staff in Wellington. The 50-watt lamp is magnified by a system of lenses and is powered by a battery supply charged by solar panels. It flashes every 12 seconds and can be seen for 19 nautical miles (35 kilometres).

Looking down on the gnarled pohutukawa which guards the entrance to the sacred cave through which, according to tradition, the spirits of departed Maori pass to their resting place. To the east is Spirits Bay where the kuaka (godwits) gather for their annual flight to breeding grounds in north-eastern Siberia and north-western America.

Graham Stewart

Graham Stewart

SHIPS THAT PASS IN THE NIGHT: In 1769 Lieutenant James Cook, after rediscovering New Zealand and claiming it for Britain, battled a hurricane in HM barque *Endeavour* while rounding the cape on his way west. Unknown to Cook, the French explorer François Marie de Surville was caught in the same hurricane while rounding the cape on the *St Jean Baptiste* after leaving the Hokianga. Somewhere north of Cape Reinga, these two famous explorers of the 18th century would have crossed paths in the storm completely unaware of each other's presence – truly one of the most believe it or not stories of all time.

Graham Stewart

The Houhora Tavern is the northernmost pub in New Zealand, 70 km south of Cape Reinga. The tavern started life as the Hukatere Hotel in 1892 near the Ninety Mile Beach. It was later dragged by teams of bullocks to Houhora when the settlement was a thriving town for gum-diggers. The addition to the building on the right dates from the early 1970s.

Houhora Hotel 1960s. A.H. & A.W. Reed, William Main collection

Brian McClintock collection

Kaitaia was once the centre of the kauri gum industry, now the farming town centre of the 'Far North'. The Maori meaning of Kaitaia is 'abundance of food', reflecting the plentiful supply of fish and shellfish from the Ninety Mile Beach.

Above: Commerce Street with the Bank of New Zealand (opened March 1915) on the corner of Bank Street when the first motorcars came to town.

Right: The present Bank of New Zealand building on the same site was opened in 1948.

Graham Stewart

'Doubtless, a bay', James Cook recorded in his journal in 1769 after considering whether it was a peninsula or an island, hence the name. Doubtless Bay was the first landfall for the legendary Polynesian explorer Kupe, according to Maori mythology, in 900 A.D. The early Maori settlers were the ancestors of the local tribe Ngatikahu who have 21 marae (meeting houses) in the Mangonui district.

With the arrival of Europeans in the 1790s, Mangonui became a whaling and trading port where kauri logs were floated down the Taipa and Oruaiti Rivers to Mill Bay and on to Mangonui for milling and export.

Alexander Turnbull Library, Northwood collection, 1/1 004909G

When horsepower had four legs – a busy scene c1910 where Beach and Waterfront Roads meet.

Brian McClintock collection

Waterfront Road is now a mecca for motels, cafe's and craft shops.

Graham Stewart

Graham Stewart

Today the settlement brings tourists to view the many heritage buildings and to dine over the water and sample the reputed best fish and chips in the land. The 3-km Mangonui heritage trail starts at the restored kauri courthouse of 1892-93, built to a standard design for small Victorian courthouses. The former post office now houses a gallery.

Whangaroa Harbour was described as 'a singular and beautiful romantic place' by British naval captain Richard A. Cruise, in 1820. It is one of the natural gems of this country with its rock pinnacles, all given biblical names, and prominent ridges of eroded volcanoes. It is now the base for boating and big-game fishing.

Whangaroa was the scene of a massacre in December 1809 when the English brig *Boyd* called to load kauri spars. Earlier visits by other ships had been given warm receptions by local Maori. It seems following the sailing of a previous ship, an epidemic had killed a number of Maori and it was suspected that the captain had placed a curse on the tribe. In mid-1808 the captain of the *Commerce* had shown his watch to Maori, which they regarded as an atua, or god, and when he accidentally dropped it into the waters of Whangaroa Harbour, they felt an unwelcome spirit had been let loose. It made them uneasy. Whangaroa chief 'George' (Te Ara) had worked his way back from Sydney on the *Boyd* as a seaman (his second period of voyaging abroad) and had been ill-treated by the captain, which added more tension. Revenge was swift: a few days after the *Boyd* weighed anchor, most of the crew were lured away to cut timber and were killed. After nightfall Maori returned to the ship and killed all except four who had been kind. About 70 perished. The next morning the ship was hauled nearer the beach, and Maori began stripping fittings from the vessel. Later in the day a striking of a flint near an opened keg of gunpowder killed several and started a fire, burning the ship down to its waterline as it drifted and grounded near Motu Wai (Red Island). This sad chapter kept European seafarers and settlers away from the area for a number of years.

Alexander Turnbull Library, 1/1 006337 G

In this early 20th century view of the Whangaroa township, to the right of the Masonic Hotel (a former boarding house) is the old town church hall, later used as the first County Council Chambers. On the hillside above the church hall are the old Whangaroa School, St Paul's Church and, far right, the school house. The church hall and St Paul's Church still stand. In the colour photograph of the town today (*right*), the pinnacle rock 'St Paul' stands aloof on the horizon behind the Marlin Hotel.

Graham Stewart

Brian McClintock collection

Keri Keri Showing Oldest Wooden and Stone Buildings in N.Z. F.G.R. 5396.

Overlooking the Kerikeri Basin is the Stone Store (left), built between 1832 and 1836 as a mission storehouse. It was built mainly of local stone, the arches, quoins and keystones were cut on the site from Sydney sandstone. The Kerikeri Mission House, Kemp House (at right), was built in 1821-1822 for the Rev. John Gare Butler, an Anglican missionary in the Bay of Islands, who had arrived in 1819 to take charge of the second mission station to be established by Bishop Marsden. The mission blacksmith, James Kemp, and his wife, Charlotte, moved into the house in 1832, and the house remained in the ownership of their descendants until 1974, the reason the house is referred to as Kemp House. The Stone Store had also passed to the ownership of the Kemp family. Both buildings are now owned by the Historic Places Trust. On the hill behind is St James Church built in 1878.

Graham Stewart

Alexander Turnbull Library, F18070 ½

Herman Schmidt, Alexander Turnbull Library, F000124211/1

Lord and Lady Bledisloe.

The Treaty House (1833) and grounds were the private property of James Busby, the British agent in New Zealand when the Treaty was signed on 6 February 1840. After years of neglect (above) the Treaty House and property were advertised for sale by the Bank of New South Wales in 1931. The Governor-General at the time, Lord Bledisloe (1867-1958), and his wife, aware of the historical importance of the estate, purchased the property in 1932 and presented it in trust to the people of New Zealand.

Graham Stewart

Alexander Turnbull Library, MNZ2746

Graham Stewart

Sir Apirana Ngata leads a haka at the opening of the meeting house beside the Waitangi Treaty House during the Treaty centennial celebrations in 1940. The meeting house symbolizes Maori involvement in the signing of the Treaty of Waitangi. The word 'runanga' means 'to discuss in assembly'.

Alexander Turnbull Library, PAcoll7756-2-0933

A place full of history, where Henry Williams established a mission station in 1823; where Government agent James Busby (1801-1871) met 22 leading Maori chiefs in May 1823; where the first substantial book was printed and published in New Zealand, William Williams' *Dictionary of the New Zealand Language*, released in 1844; where visitors can take a launch and visit some of the 144 islands in the Bay of Islands.

Graham Stewart

Alexander Turnbull Library F154770 ½

Graham Stewart

The first commercial car ferry service was started by J.C. Deeming. It was a matter of driving up the planks with guidance and care while the launch *Doris* kept the barge in position. In the 1930s the ferry operated from Paihia to Russell, before moving up-harbour to calmer waters.

Opua was once an export port for coal, frozen meat and butter, the northern terminal of the railway line from Auckland. It is now a seaside retreat with yachts for charter and the terminal of the vehicle ferry service to the other side of the bay (Okiato) which saves a 40-km drive around a winding road to Russell.

Today the vehicle ferry *Okiato* has steel ramps at each end to make the drive on and off a hassle-free exercise.

Russell. F.G.R. 504.8.

Simon Crawford collection

The original name of Russell was Kororareka, once known as the 'hell hole' of the Pacific, because of its reputation as a hotbed of lawlessness and prostitution. This tranquil holiday haven is a far cry from the 30 grog shops that once traded here. On the shores of Kororareka Bay stands the Duke of Marlborough Hotel which holds the country's first hotel licence, issued in 1840. Fires have been part of the hotel's history (1845, 1875, 1931). The present building is the fourth structure, built in 1932.

Graham Stewart

Simon Crawford collection

Graham Stewart

Scarred with musket ball holes from 1845 fighting, the Christ Church Anglican church at the corner of Church and Robertson Streets, Russell, dates from 1836. It was built by Gilbert Mair, a former ship's carpenter, with money raised by settlers, including Charles Darwin who was visiting at the time. In 1871 the roof was altered to its present configuration. The church had no name until 1873 when, at a meeting chaired by the Bishop of Auckland, the name Christ Church was adopted. The land was gifted by Maori on condition Maori and Europeans had equal rights of burial in the churchyard.

Hannah King Letheridge was the second white girl to be born in New Zealand, not the first as inscribed on her tombstone. The first white girl was Dinah Hall, although Dinah went to Australia at the age of seven and never returned. Hannah spent nearly all her long life in the Bay of Islands, dying at the age of 91 in 1907.

The launch *Alma G* trawling for game fish with distinguished guests
Earl and Countess Mountbatten on board in April 1956. The fish
were jumping that day and the guests landed a striped marlin.

The tourist launch *Kewpie Too* cruises through the
hole in the rock c1950s.

A Fullers catamaran approaches the famous hole in the rock at
Motukokako Island.

Gladys M. Goodall, Laurence Eagle collection

Brian McClintock collection

Otehei Bay became famous after being used by the American author and fisherman Zane Grey as his base camp from where he caught his first marlin in 1926. It is now a popular tourist stop where the white-sand beaches attract holidaymakers to swim, snorkel and walk the island tracks. The café on the beach is named after Zane Grey. Former British Prime Minister Sir Anthony Eden spent time here to recuperate from surgery after the Suez Canal crisis which marked a turning-point in world history.

Fullers Bay of Islands

Gladys M. Goodall, Laurence Eagle collection

Whangarei Museum and Heritage Park

Kaikohe is the centre for the farming community in the far north. The cars on the main street, named Broadway, have always been strong and sturdy to cope with the country roads in the district from the large American sedans of the 1930s to the popular 4x4s of today.

Graham Stewart

Graham Stewart

Ohaeawai is nine km from Kaikohe, a small country town at the junction of SH 1 and SH 12. The early postcard shows mail coaches about to leave the local post office. The hotel still stands on the corner, but the post office has gone – only a post box remains.

Brian McClintock collection

Mail Coaches Leaving Ohaeawai. 39.   Northwood Bros.

Brian McClintock collection

Train moving along Main St., Kawa Kawa, N.Z.

The railway line has been running down the middle of Gillies Street, the main street of Kawakawa, since the railway arrived in town in 1868. Regular train services ceased in November 1985. The Bay of Islands Vintage Railway, a community-based society, now runs a tourist railway with a 1927 steam locomotive named *Gabriel* on high days and holidays. Kawakawa also claims to have the best public toilets in the land, designed by the renowned Austrian-born artist Friedensreich Hundertwasser. The toilets opened in 1997 and have ceramic columns, bottle-glass windows, mosaic tiling, a grass roof and a real live tree.

Brian McClintock collection

Graham Stewart

Alexander Turnbull Library, APG1657½G

Kohukohu (above) in 1918, was once a thriving timber-milling town, dating from c1830 with a population that grew to over 2000 by the turn of the 20th century. Since the halcyon days, rows of elegant colonial wooden buildings have been destroyed by fire: first the hotel, then a row of stores; a hall and the library followed in 1922; in 1937 the general store and the mill; another hotel and store in 1954; then in 1967 about all that remained was felled by fire. Near the Kohukohu Bowling Club is what is claimed to be the oldest stone-arched bridge in New Zealand, built c1827. A vehicular ferry connects with Rawene every half hour from The Narrows, four km from Kohukohu.

Graham Stewart

Robin Hoare collection

Robin Hoare

Rawene is a quaint village on an arm of the Hokianga Harbour with many of its buildings perched on stilts over the water. Rawene is the third oldest place of European settlement. Its name means 'setting sun': ra means 'sun', and wene means 'setting'. Maori marched on the town in 1898 to rebel against a tax on dogs.

Above: The original town wharf shortly after it was built in the 1890s included railway lines for horse-drawn trucks to carry kauri timber from the mill to ships.

Left: The new wharf caters for pedestrians only.

Glady M. Goodall, Laurence Eagle collection

Robin Hoare

Left: An early ferry, a pontoon lashed to a launch which had room for one car, arrives at Rawene. *Above*: The Rawene-Kohukohu ferry *Kohu Ra Tuarau* is today a vital link on the Hokianga. The ferry accommodates 24 vehicles on the 15-minute crossing.

Opononi from Wharf W 280

Brian McClintock collection

A popular resort on the Hokianga Harbour which made world headlines in the summer of 1955-1956 when a friendly dolphin, given the name of Opo (after the resort), came into the harbour. During the never-to-be-forgotten summer, Opo played with the crowds, swimming around children and adults. The old double-verandah Opononi Hotel, a former gum store which became a hotel in 1918, would have been a natural grandstand to watch the fun and the frolicking Opo on the days when crowds arrived to look at this spectacle of the sea. The hotel was destroyed by fire in 1959 and replaced by a single-storey building. A.S. Andrewes and Sons general store was the centre of the community from 1871. On the foreshore a sculpture of Opo by Russell Clark is a memorial to the mammal that became a friend of the locals and was given a public burial in front of the village hall.

Graham Stewart

Kauri Museum, Matakohe

Graham Stewart

Tudor Collins (1898-1970) of Warkworth, a former kauri bushman, stands with a friend under Te Matua Ngahere 'Father of the Forest', the second-largest surviving kauri tree with the largest girth of 16.2 metres in the Waipoua Forest Sanctuary. Tudor Collins recorded with his camera the kauri industry, the men, the bush camps, the dams, the horses and bullocks, and the magnificent kauri trees of the forest. The Kauri Museum at Matakohe has the Tudor Collins Wing, opened in 1967, which houses some of his photographic collection of the kauri.

Tane Mahuta 'Lord of the Forest', the largest living kauri tree in New Zealand, is found in the Waipoua Forest Sanctuary (9113ha), in Northland, only a five-minute walk from the road that winds through this splendid forest. The Department of Conservation experts say that it is difficult to estimate the age of Tane Mahuta, but it may have sprung from seed around 2000 years ago during the lifetime of Christ. The dimensions are: trunk height 17.7 metres, total height 51.5 metres, trunk girth 13.8 metres, trunk volume 244.5 metres.

Alexander Turnbull Library, 1/1-010702G

Graham Stewart

Dargaville was named in 1887 after an early settler, Joseph Dargaville, who established a trading post there in 1872. The town, on the banks of the northern Wairoa River, first thrived on the kauri timber and gum trade, then slowly became a retail hub for the farming community. At the height of the kauri export boom, 250 ships a year entered the harbour.

Above: Victoria Street with the post office and the Northern Wairoa Hotel on each side of the intersection with Hokianga Street in 1916.

Kauri Museum, Matakohe

Roads in the winter months often became impassable, a quagmire of boggy mud. On the main road to Maungaturoto in September 1912, George Taylor's mail coach, which also doubled as the local hearse, had to be rescued during a funeral procession by Tom Coates and his bullock team.

Graham

Across the road from the museum is the Coates Memorial Church, dedicated on 27 May 1950. Joseph Gordon Coates (1878-1943) was born and educated at Matakohe. He was elected to Parliament in 1911 and was the member for Kaipara until his death in 1943. He was the first New Zealander to be appointed prime minister in 1925 when he led his party to victory.

Matakohe, the home of the renowned Kauri Museum with over 3000 square metres of displays, was founded in 1962 by Mervyn Sterling, a member of the Sterling family who were pioneer settlers in the district. The museum celebrates the kauri.

Above: In front of the original museum building, Richard Sterling gives a group of school children a ride on a four-wheeled wagon hauled by a four-horse team with a spare horse called Peggy, during the centenary celebrations of the district in 1962.

Below: The Coates Memorial Church can be seen on the horizon as horse-drawn wagons return from the centennial celebrations in 1962.

Below: The front of the Kauri Museum today.

Graham Stewart

Brian McClintock collection

Northland's only city is on the western bank of the Hatea River at the head of the Whangarei Harbour, the country's finest deep-water harbour with three ports. On Whangarei's doorstep is the Port of Whangarei; to the south is Portland, to the south-east Marsden Point. The Town Basin marina is used by the international yachting community for boat-building and maintenance. In the early years the town was isolated by inadequate roading. It was not until the 1930s, when the road to Auckland became passable in all weathers, that the town began to develop – first as an agriculture centre, then as a centre for heavy industries such as the Portland cement works and ship-building, and, in recent years, the oil refinery (opened 30 May 1964) and the oil-fired power station.

Above and below: Looking down Cameron Street, the main street of Whangarei, from the days when horse droppings on the road were a hazard for pedestrians, to when the motorcar dominated, to the pedestrian shopping mall of today with creative copper trees and a unique timeline cast in a series of bronze plaques that tell the local history as you walk the mall.

Brian McClintock collection

Graham Stewart

Simon Crawford collection

The Commercial Corner. Whangarei. F.G.R. 5808.

The first Commercial Hotel on this site was built in the 1870s and burnt down in the 1890s. The present structure was built in 1900 and was ideally placed, just along the road from the railway station when the first trains started running to Whangarei in November 1925. It was the place to stay, with a formal dining-room and all the luxuries a traveller expected in those years. It was renamed The Grand for the 1953 Royal Tour; the name Commercial was very working class in the 1950s.

Graham Stewart

Her Majesty The Queen and the Duke of Edinburgh stayed at the hotel during their tour of New Zealand in 1953-54. The hotel balcony that protrudes out onto Bank Street was ideal for the royal couple to acknowledge the welcome given to them by the citizens.

Graham Stewart

The hotel is in splendid condition and is now used for backpacker accommodation.

Waipu Museum

Waipu Museum

A settlement founded between 1854 and 1860 when 900 Scottish settlers from the Western Highlands came in six ships via Nova Scotia in Canada and Australia, led by the Rev. Norman McLeod (1780-1866). The block of land they negotiated to buy from the Government, at Waipu, was uninhabited at the time and was referred to by the Government as 'waste land'. The first small group of settlers stepped ashore at Waipu in September 1854 to start clearing the land, building shelter and creating a new homeland half a world away from their place of birth.

The focal point of the village today is over the road from the Waipu Hall, a memorial to these founders, topped proudly with the Lion of Scotland.
Left: The Coronation Hall, built in 1911, was destroyed by fire in June 1926.

Graham Stewart

A farming centre on the neck of land which connects Northland with Auckland. Rodney Street is where strip shopping (shops on both sides of a street, no malls) has been around since the first shop opened.

Above: Trams didn't ever run in Wellsford. An Auckland electric tram heads north in May 1957 on the back of a timber truck to Matakohe where the first transport museum was established in New Zealand.

Warkworth is where steamboats were the way to travel to Auckland before the metalled road was completed in the 1930s.

Above: Across the old town bridge on Elizabeth Street (c1910), under which the Mahurangi River flows, is Bridge House (*left*), built on the site of John Johnson Brown's original home, the founder of Warkworth who arrived in 1843.

Brian McClintock collection

Left: Puhoi was settled by German-speaking Bohemian peasants in 1863. The two-storeyed Colonial Puhoi Hotel was built in 1879 as the German Hotel and took over the name when the original Puhoi Hotel closed. Puhoi is only one km off State Highway One where crowds are attracted each year to the many events staged by this small community.

Graham Stewart

Graham Stewart

The Waiwera Hot Springs were New Zealand's first tourist hot-water spa attraction when built by Robert Graham in 1944. Famous for the therapeutic and curative properties of its water, it drew people from around the world to 'take the waters', bathing in and drinking the natural hot mineral water which bubbled out of the ground. The Settlers Steamship Company ran a regular service from Auckland in the 1870s. The Waiwera Hot Springs Hotel was burnt to the ground in 1939 and the wharf was dismantled shortly afterward. Today the thermal spa resort continues to attract thousands each year to relax and be rejuvenated in the thermal pools and spa.

Yvonne Coles collection

A.S. Harris, New Zealand Memories

The original bridge over the Orewa River was opened in the early 1880s. The centre section of the bridge would swing open to allow shipping to pass through. A second bridge was built in the late 1920s and served for 70 years. The present bridge opened in 1998.

Above: A woman stands by a 1920s canvas-roof baby Austin Seven motorcar with the backdrop of the original bridge in the background.

Graham Stewart

Yvonne Coles collection

In September 1880 Helensville became the busy northern railway terminus where cargo and passengers were transferred to coastal steamers for the sea voyage north over the Kaipara bar. Long gone from the main street (Commercial Road) are the roadside horse troughs, the saddlers and Big Tree motor spirits. Only 50 km from Auckland, it has become a very popular place for commuters to reside. Nearby are the Parakai hot mineral springs.

Graham Stewart

Auckland

The Tamaki area was first settled in A.D. 1400, according to historians. Before the arrival of the first European the land and the volcanic cones had been home to large numbers of Maori and their tribes. Archaeologists have discovered the isthmus was a popular area for Maori in pre-European times with its rich volcanic soil for gardening, fresh water, native pigeons and wildlife in the sub-tropical forests, and a bounty of shellfish and fish. Tribes (iwi) inhabited Maungawhau (Mt Eden) and Maungakiekie (One Tree Hill), Mangere, Mt Wellington, Mt Hobson and many other volcanic cones. From the 14th century many of the north-facing mountain slopes were terraced for use as gardens and residential areas. The isthmus was a desired area strategically, being a narrow stretch of land with an abundance of food, fertile soil and living sites, and a site of many inter-tribal wars. In 1821 Ngapuhi attacked the Tamaki people at Mokoia (near Panmure), with over 1000 deaths. This resulted in the isthmus being virtually abandoned as a residential area by Maori. By the mid-1830s small settlements were forming again. Ngati Whatua came from the north and made their headquarters at Orakei Pa in Okahu Bay. Tainui moved north and had villages at Mangere and on the area now the Auckland Domain. These people were in residence when in 1840 Europeans began to purchase land for what became Auckland city.

Yvonne Coles collection

Graham Stewart collection

On the promenade and on the sand only the children were showing their legs. A tinted postcard captures the atmosphere on a Sunday afternoon at St Heliers Bay c1910. Before the opening of Tamaki Drive in 1931, St Heliers was a long way from town: travel was either by launch or ferry, or overland by horse-bus or cart along unsealed roads past the St Thomas's ruins on the corner of Kohimaramara and St Heliers Bay Road, then on to Remuera.

The tram passenger shelter at the entrance to Mt Eden Domain on Mt Eden Road was built c1910. Electric trams started running in Pencarrow Avenue, Mt Eden, in May 1908, to Rewa Road in October 1930 and finally to Mt Albert Road in March 1931. The service closed on 22 May 1953.

Graham Stewart

Photography by Woolf

Hon. Sir Anand Satyanand (1944 -) First Governor-General of Asian and Pacific ancestry, appointed 2006. Born Auckland, educated Richmond Rd School, Sacred Heart College and the University of Auckland LLB 1970, Barrister and Solicitor 1970-1982,Government Law Reform Committee 1977-1984, Government District Court Rules Committee 1980-1982, Chairman Land Valuation Tribunal Manawatu, 1982-1985, District Licensing Committee Manawatu, 1982-1985, District Prison Board, Napier, 1985-1988, co-coordinator Judicial Orientation and Continuing Legal Education programmes District Court 1987-1994, executive member Society for Reform of Criminal Law 1991-1993, Deputy Chairman Parole Board 1992-1994, District Court Judge 1982-1994, Ombudsman 1995-2005. DCNZM 2005, PCNZM 2006, QSO 2007, GNZM 2009.

Graham Stewart

Ponsonby Road is now the trendy place to dine, enjoy a coffee or a wine and be seen while relaxing at one of the many restaurants that extend outdoors onto the pavement. In 1951 the building in the foreground was the home of the Ponsonby Car Wreckers, a bookshop that offered lay-by, a grocer who gave free home delivery and advertised Roma the dust free tea, and a boutique ice-cream shop.

Graham Stewart

NZR Publicity, New Zealand Railway & Locomotive Society collection

A little Public Works Department steam locomotive hauls filling around the bay on temporary tracks. The house in the distance sits on what is now the corner of Tamaki Drive and Watene Crescent. The building of Okahu Street up the hill to Paritai Drive has begun. Tamaki Drive, popularly known as the Waterfront Drive which skirts the harbourside cliffs, gave direct access to the seaside suburbs of Orakei, Mission Bay, Kohimarama, St Heliers and Glendowie when opened in May 1931.

Back in history, when the Ngati Whatua tribe returned from the north in the 1830s, they made the Orakei Pa in Okahu Bay their headquarters.

Graham Stewart

Graham Stewart collection

Facing page: In this c1910 view of Auckland, the vehicular ferry *Goshawk* (built 1909) is loading at the Devonport ferry terminal as the passenger ferry *Kestrel* (1905) leaves and the *Albatross* (1904) arrives from Auckland.

Mount Victoria, towering above the Auckland marine suburb of Devonport, would have witnessed a passing parade of ships from the barque *Anna Watson* which entered the Waitemata Harbour on 15 September 1840 for the founding of Auckland on Friday 18 September 1840; the first steamship built in New Zealand in 1852, the P.S. *Governor Wynyard*; the great battleships and cruise liners of each decade – the harbour ferryboats that have serviced Devonport on a regular basis since 1864 – to the grand welcome given the largest passenger liner ever to enter the harbour, *Queen Mary 2* (*below*) in February 2007.

Graham Stewart

Plans to construct a bridge to join the north and south shores of the Waitemata Harbour that had seen many proposals floated since 1860, finally came to reality when construction started in the summer of 1955 to link Westhaven with Stokes Point (Northcote). It was the last lattice girder bridge to be built in the world. On Saturday 30 May 1959 the bridge was officially opened by Governor-General Lord Cobham.

Below: To cope with Auckland's burgeoning population, four extra traffic lanes were added in 1969 (opened on 23 September). They were given the nickname of 'Nippon clip-ons'. They had been prefabricated in Japan and shipped to Auckland.

Graham Stewart

Sir Peter Blake (1948-2001). Engineer, yachtsman, adventurer. Born Auckland, educated Takapuna Grammar School, Auckland Institute of Technology 1966-69, handicap wins in legs two and four of the third Whitbread Round the World race (skipper/navigator of *Ceramco*) 1981-82, NZ Yachtsman of the Year 1982, line honours Fastnet Race (skipper of *Steinlager 2*) 1989-90, line and handicap honours in all six legs of the Whitbread Round the World race (*skipper of Steinlager 2*) Roaring Forties Trophy for best corrected time performance in legs two and three (the Southern Ocean legs) of the Whitbread Round the World race 1989-90, NZ Sports Personality of the Year 1989, NZ Yachtsman of the Year (with *Steinlager 2* crew) 1989-90, NZ Sportsman and Sports Team of the Year (with Team NZ) 1995, won Trophée Jules Verne catamaran *ENZA* 1994, British Yachtsman of the Year 1994 (with Robin Knox-Johnston), won the America's Cup *NZL 32 Black Magic* 1995, successfully defended the America's Cup 2000, blakexpeditions voyage of exploration up the Amazon and Negro rivers in Brazil 2000. MBE 1983, OBE 1991, KBE 1995.

Facing page: The clock on the ferry building reads 12.22pm and the steam ferries are bound for the North Shore on a fine summer weekend in the 1920s. *From left*: The *Makora* (built 1921) is heading for Devonport; *Ngoiro* (1913) is at the outer western ferry tee; *Pupuke* (1909) is bound for Stanley Bay; *Takapuna* (1924) is about to leave for Bayswater, and *The Peregrine* (1912) to Northcote and Birkenhead.

Graham Stewart

The ferry basin between Queens and Princes Wharves has been a busy waterway since the ferry building complex was completed in 1912. The ferry building is described as Edwardian baroque revival architecture. Ferry traffic declined with the opening of the Harbour Bridge in the early 1960s, and the future of this Auckland landmark was in question. Fortunately, the building was strengthened and renovated with the unobtrusive addition of an extra floor in the late 1980s. The ferry tower, with bells that strike the hour and half-hour, once stood prominently on the skyline until dwarfed by surrounding office tower buildings.

Below: The *Ngoiro* berths for the last timetabled run of a steam ferry to Stanley Bay on Friday 29 May 1959. After being used as a floating restaurant in the Viaduct Basin for many years, the *Ngoiro* was towed to Tairua Harbour on the Coromandel Peninsula where it was beached and used once again as a restaurant.

Hooker Bowden

Graham Stewart collection

Lower Queen Street (Queen Elizabeth Square) has always been a busy interchange for commuters arriving and leaving downtown Auckland. Regular ferry services started in the 1860s; travellers by rail arrived here when the second Auckland railway station (on the site of today's Britomart Station) opened in 1885 until it closed in 1930; horse trams started plodding to Ponsonby in 1884, followed by electric trams in 1902.

Looking up Queen Street from the old wooden Queen Street wharf in the late 1860s when the area was known as Commercial Bay. More reclamation was to follow. In the foreground are the premises of Hugh Coolahan, Bakers and Confectionery, manufacturers of ship biscuits.

Below: A horse-drawn tram waiting to leave for Newmarket in the mid-1880s: the conductor is checking his tickets on the back platform and the horses are resting. The service started in February 1886 and was extended along Manukau Road to Greenlane Road in February 1888, until replaced by electric trams in 1902.

Auckland Public library, 284

Graham Ste

During the era of the electric tram (1902-1956), many tram services terminated in Lower Queen Street. In this 1956 scene from outside Endeans building by Tyler Street, at left is the Chief Post Office, the Waverley Hotel and the Dilworth building. Palmerston building is opposite on the corner of Customs Street West and Lower Queen Street. The Oxford Theatre, known as the '*flea-pit*', is the building with the brown dome on top; to the right is Wingates hardware. Other well-known shops in this area included Hellabys the butchers, Sanfords fish shop and Sangs fruit shop on the corner of Quay Street. There were many personalities in this area, including the 'lucky' Art-Union man who sat in a small box and always wore a bowler hat and a button-hole flower. The 'peanut man' sold hot peanuts from a small street-side stall at the Quay Street corner. The sightseeing bus on the left belonged to the Auckland Bus Company.

Graham Stewart

In the latter years of the 20th century Lower Queen Street was made a pedestrian mall and named Queen Elizabeth Square. It has since reverted to a street for buses only.

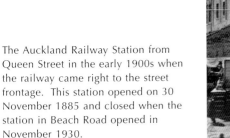

The Auckland Railway Station from Queen Street in the early 1900s when the railway came right to the street frontage. This station opened on 30 November 1885 and closed when the station in Beach Road opened in November 1930.

W.W. Stewart collection

When the Edwardian baroque-designed Central Post Office was built in 1912, the railway platforms were shortened at the Queen Street end. The base of the Post Office is Coromandel granite and the second to fourth storeys are Oamaru limestone.

Graham Stewart

Rail returned to Queen Street in July 2003 with the opening of the Britomart Station built beneath the site of the former 1885-1930 station.

Graham Stewart

Graham Stewart collection

Graham Stewart

Ellerslie racegoers waiting in Customs Street East for trams to whisk them to the racecourse c1910. On the corner of Queen and Customs Street West is the Auckland Hotel, formerly the Waitemata, an Auckland institution from 1866. The building shown was built in 1883 and demolished in 1982. Beyond is the Customhouse building completed in 1889; it was said to be the 'cheapest building of its class that had been erected in Auckland for some time past'. It still stands with dignity today. On the corner of Albert and Fanshawe Streets is the old New Zealand Loan and Mercantile Agency building which gave way to the striking West Plaza building.

Graham Stewart

Looking up Hobson Street from the intersection of Fanshawe Street. The Farmers Trading Company with the viewing tower on the roof was the equivalent to the Sky Tower of today for a view of Auckland. A children's playground on the roof of Farmers, with pedal cars and other play equipment, was always crowded. Gleesons Hotel in the foreground was a notorious pub with many 'believe it or not stories' and frequented by seamen and waterfront workers. In days past the Farmers Trading Company's building, an Auckland landmark that stood out at night when you travelled to the city by ferryboat, is now dwarfed by the Sky Tower and the massive apartment block where Gleesons Hotel once stood.

Graham Stewart

Auckland Public Library, A5572

Graham Stewart

In August 1884 the St Heliers and Northcote Land Company started the first horse-drawn tram service from the intersection of Customs Street via Queen Street, Wellesley Street West, Hobson and Pitt Streets to Karangahape Road and thence to the Ponsonby reservoir. The three-horse-drawn tram in Queen Street is approaching Wyndham Street (at left foreground); the destination reads 'Ponsonby' on the canopy above the driver.

The façade of the Bank of New Zealand building (centre), built of Hobart stone, is the only structure still standing, a timeless monument to 19th century Auckland, even though it was designed by an Australian, Leonard Terry of Melbourne, in 1865. The building was demolished in 1986 except for the façade.

TORIA S⁺ AUCKLAND.

Burton Brothers

On the site of Auckland's first gaol, the Theatre Royal building (1875), at left, which became known as the City Hall, replaced the original wooden buildings on this corner destroyed by a fire that flattened the area. In 1906 fire destroyed the City Hall and a new building, the five-storey City Chambers, was built which in turn was replaced in the early 1970s by the present National Bank of New Zealand building.

Below left: The unbelievable view of this same corner with the National Bank Towers and the Sky Tower beyond. The Sky Tower, designed by Craig Craig and Moller, and the tallest tower in the southern hemisphere, opened in December 1997.

Graham Stewart

Sir John Logan Campbell (1817-1912), 'Father of Auckland', arrived in 1839 and with his partner William Brown bought Browns Island from Maori. They started business as merchants the year the city was founded. His business interests were widespread: the first export of New Zealand produce, newspapers, shipping, banking, insurance, agriculture and his own company in the liquor trade. He was a parliamentarian, superintendent of Auckland Province and was made mayor in 1901 for the visit of the Duke and Duchess of Cornwall and York. He established a kindergarten, a crèche and an art school. He gifted Cornwall Park (93 hectares) to the city. He died on 22 June 1912 and was buried on the summit of Maungakiekie, One Tree Hill.

Wellesley Street East from the junction of Queen Street in 1903 when the pointsmen controlled tramway traffic with flags. Milne and Choyce was then on the corner where the ASB building stands today. Across the road the corner was known as Hardware Corner because Cruickshank Miller and Company was the place for Aucklanders to buy their hardware, tools and cutlery. Hardware dealers were then known as ironmongers.

On the horizon is the Auckland Public Library and Art Gallery, opened on a humid Saturday on 26 March 1887. Flags were flown from every tower on the day with the British Royal Standard flying from the clock-less main tower. The library clock was installed in 1894. The library remains as a classic piece of 19th-century architecture – early French Renaissance.

Graham Stewart collection

Dame Catherine Tizard (1931-   ). First woman mayor of Auckland (1983-1990), first woman Governor-General of New Zealand (December 1990-March 1996). Born Matamata, tutor zoology, Auckland University (1963-1983), Auckland City Councillor (1971-1983), Auckland Regional Authority (1980-1983); awarded GCMG 1990, DBE 1984, GCVO, QSO 1996.

The first woman mayor in the Auckland district was Mrs Elizabeth Yates who was elected by the citizens of the Borough of Onehunga in 1893. She also had the honour of being the first woman mayor in the British Empire – the same year as New Zealand women first voted in a parliamentary election, a first in the world.

Graham Stewart

Neil Mackenzie

Rt Hon. Helen Clark (1950-).
First elected woman Prime
Minister 1999-2008. Born
Hamilton, educated Epsom
Girls' Grammar School,
Auckland University 1968-
1976, BA 1971, MA (Hons)
1974, political studies
lecturer, Auckland University
1973-1975, 1977-1981,
elected member for Mount
Albert November 1981,
Minister of Conservation
1987-1989, Minister of
Housing 1987-1989, Minister
of Health 1989-1990,
Minister of Labour 1989-
1990, deputy prime minister
1989-1990, appointed to the
Privy Council 1990, deputy
leader of the opposition
1990-1993, leader of the
Labour Party 1993-2008,
Minister of Arts and Culture
1999-2008, United Nations
Development Programme
Administrator 2009-

Graham Stewart

The Royal George Hotel was still trading during the final month of electric trams in
December 1956. A Vauxhall Velox and a Ford Consul speed past as a tram heads
into the city via Parnell. Khyber Pass Road is on the right.
Back in 1911 a late-night tram to Onehunga coming down Khyber Pass Road parted
company from the rails at this junction and careered across the road. With only
centimetres to spare on each side, the tram ran neatly into an alleyway by the
Royal George Hotel without sustaining a scratch. With his hotel still intact, the
relieved publican opened all bars and provided drinks on the house for the shaken
passengers. The year before Halley's Comet had flashed across the sky in
spectacular fashion. It seems the motorman had fallen asleep at the controls, and
believe it or not, his name was Halley! Newmarket has become a trendy shopping
mecca of designer shops and malls.

Right: The park at the junction of
Broadway and Khyber Pass Road is
named Lumsden Green, after the
last mayor of Newmarket. The
cannon of 1880s vintage came from
North Head.

Graham Stewart

Alexander Turnbull Library, F33099½

When living in a bach on the island meant primitive conditions. The twin-screw steam ferry *Muritai* berths at Matiatia in January 1957 with holiday-makers, when travel to the island was by slow steam-driven ferries belching smoke. The *Muritai* had been built in the United Kingdom for the Eastbourne Borough Council in 1922 for their Eastbourne service in Wellington and was used as a minesweeper during the Second World War. *Muritai* was advertised as 'Auckland's largest and fastest excursion steamer with three decks, a glassed observation deck and refreshments available aboard. A great day's outing at 3/6.'

Graham Stewart

King Street c1910 from the old railway station. The original Pukekohe Hotel building on the left was handy for travellers stepping off the train in the early years. Pukekohe, with its fertile farmland and rolling hills, is known for market gardening, dairy and sheep farming. Pukekohe, surrounded by prodigious market gardens that feed Auckland, is synonymous with quality potatoes and onions throughout the land.

Alexander Turnbull Library, "001331G

Graham Stewart

Graham Stewart

When Her Majesty Queen Elizabeth II first visited New Zealand in 1953-1954, arriving on the Royal Yacht *Gothic*, the sea passage had been far from smooth. Newspapers found during the first week of the tour that the Queen was not smiling; she was not well. This all changed on the day she visited Pukekohe and this photograph was captured of a smiling Queen acknowledging acclaim there. The photograph was published around the world at the time. The bouquet was roses, carnations and maidenhair fern. The photograph was later the inspiration for a $1.20 stamp depicting Queen Elizabeth in the New Zealand Post 1950s series issued in 1994. The stamps were designed by Karen Oldham of Wellington.

Coromandel Peninsula

Thames

Alexander Turnbull Library, ½008581F

Pollen Street, showing King's Theatre, Thames

Brian McClintock collection

Thames was born when gold was discovered in the district in 1867 – it takes its name from the nearby river which Captain Cook compared to London's. At the height of gold-mining and kauri-logging in the 1860s the population was nearly double that of Auckland. It is the western gateway and the main service centre for the Coromandel.

The late Victorian wooden hotels of Thames on Pollen Street. The Brian Boru Hotel (*left*) was built in the 1868 as Reefers Arms. The hotel suffered several fires in the early years of the 20th century. The Junction Hotel (*right*) is at the other end of town on the main street. Thames boasts that Pollen Street is the longest main shopping street in New Zealand. At the height of the gold boom the town had 113 hotels.

Graham Stewart

Alexander Turnbull Library, ½001554C

The building on the left in Brown Street started life on the North Shore of Auckland in the late 1850s and was known as the 'Hylton'. In 1868 the building was barged by sea to Thames and given the name 'The Wharf' as the ferry wharf for Auckland was nearby. Another name change occurred about 1901 when the hotel was named 'The Park' after the adjacent Victoria Park. The fourth and final name change was 'The Lady Bowen'. It is now preserved as a private family home.

On the other side of the street is the elegant Bank of New Zealand building where during the mining of gold between 1868 and 1898, 67 tons of bullion, valued at $9 million in those days, was lodged. The bank moved to Pollen Street in 1926.

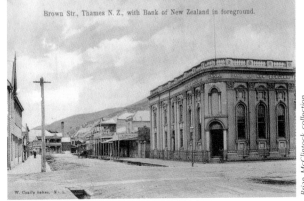

Brown Str., Thames N. Z., with Bank of New Zealand in foreground.

Brian McClintock collection

The bank building has gone as has the horse water trough on the corner of Albert and Brown Streets.

Graham Stewart

Kelvin Hynes collection

Graham Stewart

The Star and Garter Hotel on Wharf Road, Coromandel, was built c1896 and demolished in 1972. The name of the old hotel is now displayed further up the street in a romantic way on an old building (1897), formerly a drapery, converted to a bar in 2002, at the intersection of Wharf, Papanga and Tiki Roads as you arrive in town. From 1852 this old gold-mining town was named after the British naval vessel HMS *Coromandel* which anchored there in 1820 to load kauri spars.

Brian McClintock collection

Whitianga before the rows of marinas when there was only a single wharf. This safe anchorage looks out on Mercury Bay, named by Captain Cook who anchored there to observe the transit of Mercury in 1769.

Graham Stewart

W.W. Stewart collection

From the hill above the railway tunnel, the first Mercer railway station which was destroyed by fire in 1899. The hill was later removed. The railway opened to Mercer on 20 May 1875.

The second Mercer railway station and yards c1907 was built north of the township.
Below: Mercer now has an impressive motorway junction with under and overpasses. The North Island main trunk railway line can be seen in the foreground with State Highway One above. The flyover bridge is part of Mercer Ferry Road; the Waikato River is beyond.

Graham Stewart

Waikato
and the
Hauraki Plains

Princess Te Puea Herangi (1884-1952). Maori leader, founded the Turangawaewae marae in 1921, daughter of the second Maori King, Tawhiao, played an important role in the resurgence of Maori arts and crafts, Maori land rights, social welfare.

Alexander Turnbull Library, ½000977G

J.A.T. Terry collection

The Waipa Hotel at Ngaruawahia, c1910, has seen a lot of road and rail traffic pass the front door. The railway over the road arrived from Auckland in August 1877. Ngaruawahia is one of the oldest settlements in the Waikato and is where the Waikato and the Waipa Rivers merge. It is a place of importance to Waikato Maori, the Turangawaewae ('a place to stand') Marae. The official residence of the Maori King, Tuheitia Paki, is at Ngaruawahia.

Garden Place is on the left of the main street of Hamilton which is named Victoria as were many streets in New Zealand when Queen Victoria reigned (1837-1901).
Hamilton, the country's largest inland city, 129 km south of Auckland, began life as a military settlement. The city was named after Captain John Hamilton RN, who was killed at the Battle of Gate Pa. New Zealand's longest river, the Waikato, flows through the city and was Hamilton's only transport link to other towns in the region until the railway arrived in 1877.

Graham Stewart

New Zealand Herald

From 1884 to September 1964 road traffic on Victoria Street, Hamilton, had to give way to railway traffic. Hamilton had celebrated its 20th birthday with a population of just over 1200 people when the line opened, and with only two trains a day crossing Victoria Street, congestion was not a problem. When the railway was extended to Rotorua and Thames, delays at the level crossing were a concern, and as early as 1912 the Hamilton Borough Council started to lobby for the line to be lowered. It was not until the 1960s that a new low-level concrete bridge was built to carry the railway line and the old railway bridge converted for motor traffic, becoming part of Claudelands Road.

Graham Stewart

Merle Sneddon collection

K.B. Ward

The old railway bridge started life with only two pairs of cast-iron cylinder piers and concrete piers at each end for support. When heavier steam locomotives were built, the bridge had to be strengthened and an extra cast-iron cylinder was added on each side of the river in 1908. At the same time a walkway was opened after decades of protests from Claudelands residents.

James Taylor collection

The old Cambridge post office across the road from the roundabout at the junction of Victoria and Duke Streets is now the GPO Bar and Brasserie with tables and umbrellas on the pavement. The clock tower and the tall chimney have gone but not the inscription over the main entrance 'E vii R 1908' which is proudly displayed. Cambridge has an English country atmosphere with shady European trees, band rotundas and a village green. Like Hamilton, it began life as a military settlement. The town was named after the garrison's commander-in-chief, the Duke of Cambridge, not the British university town. Thoroughbred horse studs in the district have bred some of New Zealand's famous racehorses.

Graham Stewart

Alexander Turnbull Library, ½001053G

Raglan's Bow Street in July 1904, before the planting of the palm trees, shows the Harbour View Hotel (centre right) which has been a popular meeting place for over 140 years with its Verandah Bar, Historic Bar, Sports Bar and the Garden Bar. It is the second structure on the site, the first built in 1866 was burnt to the ground, leaving only the chimneys standing in 1901. It was rebuilt to the original plans in 1902. *Lower left*: A busy scene showing the second Harbour View Hotel in the early years of the 20th century.

Settled by Europeans in the mid-1850s, the town was named after Lord Raglan who was the commander of British forces in the Crimean War.

Graham Stewart

Bruce and Cilla White, NZ Memories

Graham Stewart

Alexander Turnbull Library, ½006266G

The Commercial Hotel (above left) on Alexandra Street, c1908, has been part of the fabric of Te Awamutu since the late 1870s in many guises. This dairy-farming community is a few kilometres north of the King Country where the first North Island cooperative dairy factory was established in 1882 after the railway had opened in 1880. It was an isolated settlement until the tribal disputes with the King Country's Maori chiefs were settled and before the railway arrived.

Graham Stewart

Simon Crawford collection

The Domain. Te Aroha. F.G.R. 4808.

At the base of Mount Te Aroha (952m) is the old Cadman bathhouse building (1898) where people flocked from the 1890s to 'take the waters' at the therapeutic hot springs. The building now houses the Te Aroha and District Museum. The Te Aroha mineral pools still function and are open every day. It is a rural town in the Thames Valley, with the world's only hot soda water geyser close by at Mokena.

Graham Stewart

The Nottingham Castle Hotel, c1916, with long spectacular balconies at the junction of Thames and Studholme Streets, like many hotels has been through a fire and risen again from the ashes. It was originally built in 1876 and burnt down in 1913. The township of Morrinsville was established against all odds on low-lying land that required extensive drainage in the early years.

The clock tower on Broadway, Matamata, erected in November 1964, was a gift to the town from the local Lions Club. It has since been moved to the centre of the Broadway-Arawa Street intersection, in the heart of this dairy community. Just out of town are the remains of the Hobbiton set, home of the Hobbits used in the *Lord of the Rings* series of films.

Left: Paeroa's Belmont Road c1918 when, without the fear of traffic, children could play on the street. Situated on the edge of the Hauraki Plains and once a major port on the Ohinemuri River, the town is best known for the household drink 'Lemon and Paeroa', 'L&P', made from local mineral water with lemon added. The drink is no longer made in the town of its birth.

Alexander Turnbull Library, Fred E. Flatt, ½000534G

Graham Stewart

Right: Miners outside the union hall during the long and bitter 1912 Waihi strike which lasted five months and ended with a miner being killed. The Martha Mine above the town where gold was discovered in 1878 was one of the richest gold strikes in the country. The Rob Roy Hotel over the road in the photograph was built by Orkney Islander John Flett in 1896 and has largely remained unchanged. In 1908 the town voted itself dry at the liquor polls in protest at liquor prices charged by the breweries. It became illegal to buy or sell alcohol in Waihi until restoration in 1925. During the dry years, illegal stills and home-brewing plants were often raided by police. The town is at the southern end of the Coromandel Peninsula.

Alexander Turnbull Library, PAcoll 5792-05

Graham Stewart

The King Country

Government Accomodation House, Waitomo. F.G.R.4426.

Graham Stewart collection

Christine Johnson collection

TRAVEL by RAIL

Follow the Sun
NEW ZEALAND RAILWAYS

WHERE TO GO SERIES

FAIRY CAVES OF WAITOMO

Nonpareil Service Zealous Staff Reliable Always

Graham Stewart

The Waitomo Caves – this natural underground wonder formed more than 30 million years ago, contains the Glowworm, Aranui and Ruakuri limestone caves where the stalactites, stalagmites and sculptures have developed over thousands of years. Visitors can take a boat trip through the one-metre-high Cathedral Cavern, where opera diva Kiri Te Kanawa once sang. The caves were first explored in 1887 by local Maori Chief Tane Tinorau and English surveyor Fred Mace. Local Maori knew of the caves but the subterranean caverns had never been investigated. By 1889 Tane Tinorau had opened the caves to tourists. Wai in Maori means 'water' and tomo 'hole or shaft'. The historic Waitomo Caves Hotel was originally built by the government as an accommodation house. The first motorcars did not reach Waitomo until 1922. Waitomo is 16 km south-west of Otorohanga.

Alexander Turnbull Library, 1/2000781G

The King Country was where Kingite Maori lived in semi-hostile isolation after they retreated in defeat following the Waikato conflict. For nearly 20 years it was banned territory for Europeans until the Maori King Tawhiao in 1884 made peace. Otorohanga was a major Maori settlement in the mid-19th century and when white settlers arrived in the 1880s, it became a trading post on the Waipa River followed by an invasion of labourers working on the North Island main trunk and timber millers. Maniapoto Street (*above*) c1900s, before tarseal and parking restrictions, before the street was decorated with the murals and displays of Kiwiana: pavlova, gumboots, Marmite and buzzy bees.

Graham Stewart

Alexander Turnbull Library, F.G. Smith, ½045811G

Te Kuiti, known as New Zealand's sheep-shearing capital, where the New Zealand sheep-shearing championships are held each year, started its European life as a railway construction camp. The Maori King Tawhiao made the settlement his headquarters for 17 years from 1864 to 1881 after the Battle of Orakau, living in the village of Te Kuititanga. He gave Te Kooti shelter here in 1872, where Te Kooti remained until given a pardon in the early 1880s. The main street, Rora Street c1920 (*left*), runs level with the railway line.

Graham Stewart

Alexander Turnbull Library, F.G. Smith, ½005822F

Taumarunui, once a Maori village, is at the southern end of the King Country on the upper reaches of the Whanganui River at the junction of old canoe routes. When the area opened to Europeans in the 1880s, it took three days by riverboat to reach Wanganui. Much folklore has been written about Taumarunui and its association with the main trunk railway which opened with the first express trains between Auckland and Wellington in February 1909. The line between Te Kuiti and Taumarunui had opened in 1903.

Above right: The main street, c1914, is named Hakiaha, here viewed from opposite the railway station.

Graham Stewart

Alexander Turnbull Library, PAcoll 5932-30

Ohinemutu Rotorua, N.Z.   80   W. J. ROBINSON'S PHOTO

The historic lakeside thermal village of Ohinemutu where today's Rotorua was born as a town for tourists visiting the 'hot lakes' in the 1880s. St Faith's Anglican Church (1914) stands on land leased from Ngati Whakaue   Although Tudor in style on the outside it is decorated in Maori tradition within. Across Lake Rotorua (Te Rotorua nui a Kahumatamomoe) is Mokoia Island on the horizon.

Graham Stewart

Rotorua
and the
Bay of Plenty

Rotorua Museum of Art and History, Te Whare Taonga o Te Arawa,NZ,OP1131

Merle Sneddon collection

A 1920s motorbus in front of the Prince's Gate at the Arawa Street entrance to the Government Gardens, Rotorua. The arches were originally erected for the visit of the Duke and Duchess of Cornwall in 1901 at the junction of Fenton and Hinemoa Streets, hence the name Prince's Gate.

You can no longer park your horse and cart under the palm trees on The Strand (originally called Beach Road) near the intersection of Wharf Street on the waterfront at Tauranga. The Masonic Hotel (1866) with the large colonial verandah (right) was demolished in 1993.

Graham Stewart

Whakarewarewa Village is home to the Tuhourangi Ngati Wahiao people, where since the mid-1800s they have hosted people from all parts of the world to view the bubbling mud pools, boiling mineral springs, silica terraces and the erupting geysers, all part of the natural wonders.

Glays M. Goodall, William Main collection

Graham Stewart

The archway at the entrance to the Whakarewarewa Village is a memorial to their kinsfolk who served and those who gave their lives in both world wars and in South-East Asia.

Below: Early hand-coloured Victorian postcards c1900s show people watching the 'soaping the Wairoa Geyser' and a view of the Maori village within the geothermal wonders of Whakarewarewa where Maori live in and around hot mud that simmers and spits, where the earth's crust is so dangerously thin.

Graham Stewart collection

Whakarewarewa, Rotorua

Graham Stewart collection

DIVING FOR PENNIES, WHAKAREWAREWA, ROTORUA N.Z.

The old bridge at the entrance to the Whakarewarewa Maori Village at Rotorua where for many generations Maori children dived for coins thrown by tourists into the sulphur-coloured river.

Graham Sstewart

The entrance arch and bridge to Te Puia on Hemo Road, Rotorua, is the Maori cultural centre where Maori song and dance, the traditional welcome, the challenge, the poi dance, Maori stick games and the male war dance, the haka, are staged. There is a kiwi house and workshops for weaving and cooking in hot pools.

Jean Batten was born in Rotorua on 15 September 1909 – she was the first woman to make the return flight from England to Australia and to cross the South Atlantic and the Tasman Sea. The people of Rotorua named her 'Hine-o-te-Rangi', daughter of the skies. Jean Batten died on 22 November 1982 in Palma, Majorca. There is a fitting memorial to her in the gardens of the Rotorua City Centre, and at the Auckland International Airport her famous Percival Gull 6 aircraft is on permanent display together with a bronze statue.

Merle Sneddon collection

Rotorua is the heartland of the Arawa tribe. The Arawa people are tangata whenua (original inhabitants) of the Rotorua district. It was New Zealand's first tourist town, a city on the boil with the smell of hydrogen sulphide and steam rising from street gratings. There are a number of impressive geysers. The best known geyser, Pohutu ('big splash' or 'explosion'), which shoots hot water 30 metres into the sky, is at the Te Whakarewarewa geothermal valley on the southern outskirts of the town.

Above and below: Tutanekai Street is one of the many shopping streets in the centre of town.

Graham Stewart

Simon Crawford collection

Renamed the Tudor Towers in the 1950s, this gem of Tudor-style architecture with Royal Dalton baths when built, was the New Zealand Government's first investment in the tourism industry and was opened on 13 August 1908. The Bath House, 'The Great Spa of the South Seas' as the building was once known, brought people worldwide to the curative powers of the mineral waters. The building is a national treasure and now houses the Rotorua Museum of Art and History. The Government Gardens around the museum have croquet lawns, bowling greens, petanque green and rose gardens as well as steaming thermal pools.

Graham Stewart

Graham Stewart collection

Tauranga – the name means 'resting place' or 'safe anchorage' – is one of New Zealand's fastest growing cities, a busy export port and centre of the kiwifruit industry. The Strand (*above and below*) is a waterfront strip of palms and parklands on the foreshore of Waipu Bay, the town's front window. Only five km from the city centre is the site of the Battle of Gate Pa on Cameron Road where St George's Church (1899) stands, and where local Maori defeated the British colonial forces on 29 April 1864.

Graham Stewart

Wayne Ward

The ferry *Kestrel* served Auckland for 80 years and is still in demand, as the floating seafood 'Kestrel at the Landing' restaurant on the waterfront at Tauranga. The steam ferry *Kestrel* was built and launched in Auckland in December 1905. When the victorious All Blacks arrived home in March 1906 from Britain to a tumultuous welcome, it was the new ferry *Kestrel* that carried them from the liner *Sonoma* to the civic reception at the city ferry tee. The *Kestrel* serviced Aucklanders through two world wars and in the early 1950s was converted from a steam-driven ferry to diesel power. As a motor ship, she was to continue in service until sold in 2001 to the present Tauranga owners for conversion into a floating restaurant.

Graham Stewart

Right: 'The Mount' stands at the entrance to Tauranga Harbour, with a scattering of holiday baches and Maunganui Road running down the centre of the peninsula – in 1932 the only road to the Mount Mauao Reserve and the 1.5-kilometre walking track around Mauao. On the right is the internationally known ocean surf beach on the Pacific Ocean and on the left the sheltered harbour, popular for swimming and water sports. The view below from the Mount Drury Reserve of this popular holiday and retirement centre gives a panoramic view of the modern apartment tower blocks, residential and holiday homes of today.

Alexander Turnbull Library, ½071287F

Graham Stewart

Above left: Looking down Wharf Street, Tauranga, c1910, towards the Coronation Pier on The Strand.

Left: The scene today.

Graham Stewart

Merle Sneddon

Graham Stewart

Te Puke is 23 km south-east of Tauranga. This rich horticultural area was first settled by Ulstermen in the latter half of the 19th century and is known as the kiwifruit capital of the world, where this fruit was first planted commercially. The Te Puke Hotel, c1906, still stands on Jellicoe Street in the town.

Alexander Turnbull Library, F022283 ½

Graham Stewart collection

Whakatane, with its natural harbour at the mouth of the Whakatane River in the eastern Bay of Plenty, is where you can see steam rising from the active crater lake on White Island on the horizon. White Island is New Zealand's most active volcano. Whakatane is within reach,11 km, of Ohope ocean beach. The arrival of Maori goes back over 1000 years to Tiwakawaka and then Toi. The descendants founded Kapu-te-rangi, one of the oldest known pa sites. 200 years after the Toi people arrived, the last great migration saw the arrival of Toroa, captain of the waka (canoe) *Mataatua,* and his people. European settlement began in the 1830s with the arrival of the first whalers and missionaries.

Graham Stewart

Graham Stewart

Eastland

Opotiki was an important port and settlement in the early days – today it is the entrance to the East Cape and Eastland – the eastern gateway to the Bay of Plenty.

Above: The Masonic Hotel at the junction of Church and Elliott Streets, Opotiki, c1910, suffered fires in 1865 and 1919. The third generation building (*below*) is an elegant hostelry.

Right: The Royal Hotel on the corner of King Street and the main street of Opotiki was built in 1886 and is the original structure. It is now Hunters Backpackers.

Alexander Turnbull Library, ¼001069F

Te Kaha was an old whaling settlement where the Whanau-a-Apanui people used to row out in pursuit of migrating whales. The last catch was hand-harpooned in 1925. The district gets its name from the many sieges by invading tribes they withstood. Te Kaha means 'to stand firm'.

Above: The general store in July 1944 where locals would call for supplies and a yarn. The old Te Kaha Hotel is behind.

Below: The Te Kaha Beach Resort (2008), built on the site of the old hotel, includes a restaurant with a panoramic view of the Pacific Ocean.

Graham Stewart

Graham Stewart

Graham Stewart

Graham Stewart

The Raukokore Anglican Church was built by settler Duncan Stirling in 1894 and stands on a promontory close by the rocky foreshore in Papatea Bay. The first wedding ceremony at the church was when Duncan Stirling married Mihi Kotukuku in 1896.

Shades of the loaves and the fishes – in recent years a colony of penguins has made its home under the church which at times creates a very fishy smell within.

Right: The wharf at Hicks Bay was used by coastal steamers until the mid-1960s when the sea was the only corridor for transportation of produce. The Richardson and Company coaster, SS *Pakura* (1924-61), berthed at the wharf in 1924. Today the wharf is popular as a platform for casting the rod. The bay, originally named Te Wharekahika, was renamed by Captain James Cook in 1769 after a crew member on the *Endeavour*.

D.C. Sheppard

'It used to be said that Richardsons' ships would go anywhere cargo could be had. Certainly, open beaches, creeks, bays and exposed roadsteads were all part of a day's work for its ships and crews for more than a hundred years' – Gavin McLean, author of the book *Richardsons of Napier*, 1989.

Gray Clapham

Gladys M. Goodall, William Main collection

Alexander Turnbull Library, ¼000661F

Te Araroa, on Kawakawa Bay under the escarpment of Whetumataerau (*upper right* – October 1943), is where the legend that inspired the book and film *Whale Rider* originated from and also the birthplace of Sir Apirana Ngata who was a Member of Parliament for 38 years. Only 22 km to the east is the East Cape lighthouse, the most easterly tip of New Zealand. In the school grounds is Te Waha-o-Rerekohu, the world's oldest and largest pohutukawa tree with a girth of 20 metres, reputed to be over 600 years old.

Graham Stewart

Ruatoria, centre of the Ngati Porou tribe, is a short detour off State Highway 35, 150 km north of Gisborne. The Manutahi Hotel has been around for over 80 years and is a popular meeting place in the village known as the 'capital city' of the East Coast.

Tikitiki – was the home of Pine Taiapa (1901-1972), the great Maori carver of the modern period.

Below: St Mary's Anglican Church, built in 1924 and consecrated in 1926, commemorates members of the Ngati Porou tribe who died in the First World War. The ornate interior of Maori carvings and woven panels was created by local Ngati Porou crafts people; the pulpit was a gift from the Te Arawa tribe. On the east wall is a memorial to Sir Apirana Ngata. It was the first building worked on by the master carver Pine Taiapa.

Merle Sneddon collection

MAIN STREET, RUATORIA

Alexander Turnbull Library. ½045105F

Graham Stewart

ST COAST.

Alexander Turnbull Library, PAcol 779674

Graham Stewart

Tokomaru Bay was once a busy coastal township before the Tokomaru Sheep Farmers' Freezing Company's works closed in 1952. At the eastern end of the bay was a wharf from where produce was exported, when the sea was the main highway out of town.

Above: The post office building, c1910, is now the Te Poutapeta Bed and Breakfast.

Graham Stewart

Graham Stewart

Alexander Turnbull Library, PAcol 0196244

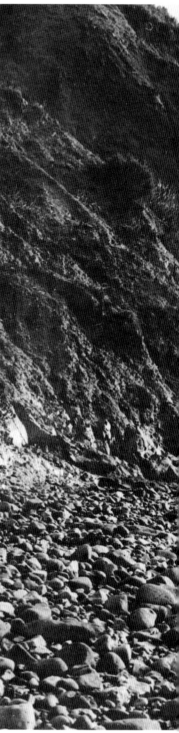

Tolaga Bay, just north at Anaura Bay, is where James Cook had his first friendly meeting with Maori in October 1769. The streets in the town are named after Cook's crew. In the days of coastal shipping the wharf was designed so ships could load whether the tide was low or high. The country's longest wharf was built in 1926-29 and is about 660 metres; the wharf was officially opened on 22 November 1929. The port was closed for shipping in 1968.

Graham Stewart

Two horse-drawn coaches moving south along the rocky foreshore near Tolaga Bay in the 1880s. It is hard to imagine that the smooth surface of State Highway 35, known today as the Pacific Coast Highway, is a dream to drive compared with the days when the horses had mud up to their knees on the inland parts of the road and had to negotiate the rocky, uneven surface on the coastal sections. To lighten the load for the horses, passengers travelling by horse-drawn coaches often walked over the problem sections.

On 9 October 1769 Captain James Cook was rowed from HM barque *Endeavour* with botanist Joseph Banks by crew members and stepped ashore on Kaiti Beach where Gisborne is today. Cook wanted to replenish the ship's supplies. When traditional challenges were misunderstood, skirmishes happened and Maori were killed. Cook sailed without provisions, regretting he had not been able to establish cordial relations, and thus Poverty Bay received its name.

Left: A statue of Cook in an admiral's uniform he never wore was placed on Kaiti Hill during the bicentenary celebrations of Cook's landing. The uniform is not that of the British Navy, and since October 1969 the statue has been a source of embarrassment for historians.

Above: A more authentic statue of James Cook is at the corner of Customhouse Street and Awapuni Road near the mouth of the Turanganui River. It is a sculpture by New Zealander Anthony Stones and was presented to the city in March 2000. It stands on a granite globe that maps Cook's three Pacific voyages.

Gisborne

Simon Crawford collection

Gisborne – where European history in New Zealand began – is the most easterly city in the world, close to the International Date Line. It is a prosperous centre, despite being in 'Poverty Bay', with food production, forestry and viticulture together with a Mediterranean climate. Gladstone Road is the heart of the city with continuous shops on both sides of the road. In the distance beyond the tram can be seen the old post office tower which for years was a Gisborne landmark. The old post office clock is now housed in the Robinson Memorial Clock Tower in the middle of Gladstone Road.

Graham Stewart

Alexander Turnbull Libray, S.C. Smith, 45594½

In 1913 the Gisborne Corporation installed the first battery-propelled tramway system in the southern hemisphere which did not require trolley-poles or overhead wires. The trams were battery-propelled at 16 kilometres an hour. The service ran from the Customhouse Street junction, along Gladstone Road to Roebuck Road; in 1915 the service was extended to Stanley Road and in September 1918 to Lytton Road. When the Peel Street bridge opened in November 1923, a new line was laid along Peel Street, Fitzherbert Street and Ormond Road to Whataupoko. Sadly, the trams never paid their way and were always a burden on the ratepayers until the system closed on 8 July 1929.

Graham Stewart

Graham Stewart collection

The crowds gathered at the opening of the new Peel Street bridge in November 1923, and the first vehicle across the bridge ahead of the fire brigade was a battery tram loaded with local dignitaries. The original name of Gisborne was Turanga-nui-a-Kiwa. Europeans began settling in Turanga in 1831, but as confusion between Tauranga and Turanga was causing problems, it was renamed Gisborne in 1872, after the New Zealand colonial secretary William Gisborne.

Graham Stewart

Taupo is on the northern shores of Lake Taupo (623 sq km), a lake the size of Singapore. It was formed by massive volcanic eruptions between 50,000 and 22,000 years ago. The lake is named for the ancestor Tia's rain cloak (taupo); the full name is Te Taupo nui a Tia. It is also called Taupo moana (Taupo sea). Europeans first discovered the lake area in the 1830s, but few settled as the land was not suited for farming. Trout were introduced to the lake in the early years of the 20th century, brown trout 1895 and rainbow trout 1905. In 1922 the ownership of the lake bed was returned to Ngati Tuwharetoa.

Alexander Turnbull Library, PAcol 593220

Looking out onto Lake Taupo from the junction of Tongariro Street and Tuwharetoa Street.

Graham Stewart

Alexander Turnbull Library, Eph E Tourist

A 1930s advertisement telling the world about trout fishing on Lake Taupo.

From a sleepy lakeside road-stop, Taupo has mushroomed in the last 50 years to become a thriving tourist town. European settlement began when the Armed Constabulary built a redoubt in 1869 during the East Coast land war (1868-72) as defence against Te Kooti. The thermal water baths they established still carry their name, the A.C. (Armed Constabulary) Baths, now part of the Taupo Events Centre.

Taupo

and

the Volcanic Plateau

Alexander Turnbull Library, PA10229204

Graham Stewart collection

The entrance to the Wairakei Hotels past and present. The Bayview Wairakei Resort Hotel, now a modern tourist facility, is a former Government Tourist Corporation hotel.

The famous historic Terraces Hotel, Taupo (1889), named after the black silica terraces that once surrounded it, is on the Napier Taupo Road beside the Taupo DeBretts Spa Resort. It is now a modern boutique hotel named Peppers Terraces Resort Lake Taupo Hotel.

Graham Stewart

Taupo Museum

Tongariro Street when service stations were always positioned on street corners. In this 1930s scene only one motorcar is moving on the street. The planning of such a wide thoroughfare has paid dividends for Taupo, now a magnet for visitors, with so much to offer at its front door – from fishing for rainbow and brown trout, skydiving, jet-boating and bungy-jumping to visiting all the natural attractions such as the nearby thunderous Huka Falls.

Graham Stewart

Graham Stewart collection

The lake's outlet, where the mighty Waikato River is born – the longest river in New Zealand – 425 km from the headwaters to the Tasman Sea. Waikato means 'flowing water'.

The waters from Mount Ruapehu descend to Lake Taupo where they feed the lake at the southern end and leave at the northern end, then down through the Huka Falls at an alarming pace to the Aratiatia Rapids and on through other hydro-electric power stations from Arapuni to Karapiro. In central Waikato the river flows at a gentle pace past Cambridge and through the heartland of Hamilton to the Waipa River at Ngaruawahia. It then passes Huntly, Mercer, Rangiriri and Meremere, low-lying land where flooding often happens, and finally reaches the Tasman Sea.

Graham Stewart

J.A. Murphy collection

Bayview Chateau Tongariro

Bayview Chateau Tongariro

Alexander Turnbull Library, Eph-E-tourism-ca1932 01

In 1887 the paramount chief of the Ngati Tuwharetoa tribe gifted to the people of New Zealand the Tongariro National Park, including the mountains of Ruapehu, Ngauruhoe and Tongariro. The park now covers 79598 hectares and in 1990 became a World Heritage area. Ruapehu and Tongariro are still active volcanos. In 1929 the Chateau Tongariro, styled after the Canadian resort at Lake Louise, was built alongside the original Whakapapa Chateau on the slopes of Mt Ruapehu. When the hotel celebrated its 75th birthday, the name was changed to Bayview Chateau Tongaririo.

Facing page: Shortly after the Chateau opened, sightseeing cars operated by Tongariro Tourist Motors prepare to depart with tourists.
Above: A colour poster promoting travel by rail to the Chateau c1932.

Bayview Chateau Tongariro

John MacCready collection, courtesy NZ Memories

John MacCready collection, courtesy NZ Memories

State Highway One across the bleak, barren tussock plateau on the eastern side of the Tongariro National Park has not always been a smooth ride – back in the early days there could be mud up to the axles, sometimes requiring more than one attempt to negotiate a boggy, clay section or to ford water at an unknown depth – both can be seen in the photographs.

Graham Stewart

Merle Sneddon collection

Standing 800 metres above sea level, Waiouru is often referred to as the Siberia of the land because of the extreme bitter winters experienced on this exposed plateau. It is the home of the Army's training camp and the National Army Museum, Te Mata Toa, where the military history of New Zealand is displayed. It is the highest railway station above sea level on the New Zealand railway network.

Graham Stewart

Graham Radcliffe collection

Above: Raurimu c1917, 50 km south of Taumarunui, is at the foot of the unique spiral on the North Island main trunk, a railway engineering feat of the early 20th century. It conquered the impossible, taking the railway line from the settlement of Raurimu, climbing 215 metres in just 11 km round three horseshoe curves with the line crossing over itself in a complete circle through two tunnels up to the central volcanic plateau. The steepest gradient is 1 in 50. Bill Pierre tells the story in his book *North Island Main Trunk* of a locomotive driver in the early days who told of his consternation on seeing red tail lights ahead and brought his long goods train to an emergency stop. On investigation he found that he had merely caught up with his own guard's van!

Graham Stewart

Merle Sneddon collection

Gladys M. Goodall, Laurence Eagle collection

Ohakune, known as the carrot capital of New Zealand, was just a milling and market-gardening town until the advent of the Turoa Ski Fields only 17 km away on the Ohakune Mountain Road. The town is now a bustling accommodation centre for skiers who flock to the slopes.

Above left: Looking like a wild west town, the mud-sodden main street of Ohakune before the railway arrived in town, early 1900s.

Graham Stewart

New Zealand Herald, Noel Bennett

Mount Ruapehu looms above the wreckage of the Wellington-to-Auckland express that plunged into a roaring torrent of lahar floodwater, sweeping down the Whangaehu River at Tangiwai on Christmas Eve, 24 December 1953. Minutes before the express arrived at the Whangaehu River railway bridge, the sudden discharge of thousands of tonnes of water from the crater lake had sent a giant 6 metre (20 ft) roaring wave on a path of destruction. This great surge of water carried away the massive concrete piers of the railway bridge, wrecked the adjacent road bridge and swept on to smash down three smaller bridges near the coast. It was the fifth-worst disaster in New Zealand's history.

Graham Stewart

KA 949 NZGR

NUMBER PLATE
OF THE
WELLINGTON
TO
AUCKLAND
EXPRESS
24TH DECEMBER 1953

Rangitikei, Manawatu & Wanganui

Alexander Turnbull Library, ¼027526F

Taihape.N.Z. Main Road 1342. F.G.R.

Alexander Turnbull Library, ½007078G

Taihape, since the arrival of Canterbury settlers and a railway construction camp during the building of the North Island main trunk, has developed as a farming centre. It is perched high on the edge of the volcanic plateau, above the surrounding river gorges. As most of the locals wear gumboots on the farm and into town, it has become known as the Gumboot Capital of the World.

Above: The 1907 post office c1918, when the clock tower stood high on Hautapu Street.
Above right: Hautapu Street when it was a metal and muddy thoroughfare.

Graham Stewart

Noel Meek

The 1980s saw many deviations on the North Island main trunk railway, in preparation for the electrification of the 411 km between Palmerston North and Te Rapa (Hamilton). Major civil engineering work between Marton and Taumarunui included alterations to tunnels, bridges and station yards, together with curve and grade easements.

One of the larger deviations occurred near the rural locality of Mangaonoho, 26 km south-west of Taihape in the Rangitikei. Originally opened in April 1893, this section, known as the 'Mangaonoho Bank', included steep grades, sharp curves, a narrow tunnel and a sweeping horseshoe curve. The deviation, opened in August 1985, shortened the line and bypassed the tunnel and horseshoe with its speed-restricting curves.

Above: A southbound train snakes around the curves at the north end of the old alignment in April 1985.

Below: An electric locomotive climbs the steeper, but straighter, Mangaonoho deviation in February 2002.

Graeme Jupp

Merle Sneddon collection

J.A.T. Terry collection

The once busy part of Mangaweka was Broadway with a two-storey Bank of New Zealand branch on the corner of Kawakawa Street and the Langholm Hotel nearest the camera. The railhead reached here in November 1902, then two years passed before the line from Mangaweka to Taihape opened in November 1904. 22 km south of Taihape, State Highway One now bypasses the old main street, and with the opening of the Mangaweka Utiku railway deviation in November 1981, the railway was also taken away from the township.

Construction of the Makohine viaduct near Ohingaiti on the North Island main trunk line began in 1897 and was completed in 1902. The engineer responsible for the design was Peter Seton Hay of the Public Works Department who also designed the Mangaweka and Matatote railway viaducts. He also designed the Hapuawhenua, Taonui and Maunganui o te Ao viaducts but did not live to see them built, as he died of pneumonia in 1907. The Makohine viaduct was the first major engineering structure built by the Public Works Department. The viaduct was later strengthened by having additional bracing inserted in the trusses.

Graham Stewart

Hunterville, named after an early settler by the name of George Hunter, was founded in 1884 as a small timber and railway town in the heart of the Rangitikei district and has over the years become a sheep-farming centre. The old Taylors general store has been on the main street since 1904.

In the early years of the 20th century before the North Island main trunk opened in 1908, roads were basic tracks that quickly became muddy quagmires in wet weather with horses sinking into the bogs. A horse and trap would take about three hours to reach Mangaweka from Hunterville.

Marton was named in 1869 on the centenary of Cook's landing in New Zealand after Captain James Cook's birthplace in the United Kingdom, where he was born on 27 October 1728. Marton in the United Kingdom is 32 km from the Port of Whitby from where Cook first ventured out to sea. The town had earlier been called Tutaenui.

Above: The main street of Broadway c1924, with a mix of historic commercial buildings, is the service centre of the Rangitikei district founded in the 1860s. It is known for three private boarding schools: Nga Tawa, Huntley and Turakina Maori Girls' College.

Graham Stewart collection

Feilding was first colonised in January 1874 as part of the Manchester Block purchased from the Wellington Provincial Government. The town was named after Lieutenant-Colonel William Feilding, a director of the Emigrants and Colonists Aid Corporation Ltd. The town clock tower in Manchester Square today is modelled on the clock tower of the old post office which was built in the early years of the 20th century and opened by Sir Joseph Ward, then postmaster general, on 27 February 1902. The town clock was not installed in the post office tower until 1904. When the building was damaged in the June 1942 earthquake, it was demolished and a new post office built on the same site in 1949. Fortunately, the town clock had been placed in storage for 56 years and was reinstated when the freestanding tower was built in 1998 as part of the Manawatu District Millennium Project.

Graham Stewart

Palmerston North, known by Maori as Papaioea 'how beautiful', was just a clearing in the Manawatu forest when first visited by Europeans in 1846. Maori sold the land to the crown in 1864 and the first settlers arrived in 1866. It was to become the main city of the Manawatu region, with a central 7-hectare square surveyed in 1866 which is today the focal point of the town. The city was named after Lord Palmerston, a British statesman in the 19th century, the 'North' being added to distinguish it from Palmerston in the South Island in 1873. The city is the home of Massey University.

Below: The New Plymouth express passing through The Square in the 1920s.

New Plymouth Express passing through Square. Palmerston North. To

Alexander Turnbull Library, ¼048702F

The Square with its grassy areas was a divided place from the 1870s until October 1963 with the railway line running through the middle of the city, leaving a mantle of smoke as each train passed.

Left: City Council-owned motorbuses and the post office when the clock tower was the tallest structure in town, c1925.

All Saints Anglican Church (1914) and the Grand Hotel (1906) at the south-west corner of The Square with a miniature lake in the foreground. The lake was built by the council in 1909 in the shape of a butterfly with outspread wings, the 'body' of the butterfly being the bridge which has been rebuilt in recent years. The Grand Hotel closed in 1972 and now houses shops and offices. All Saints Church was designed by Frederick de Jersey Clere of Wellington. The cannon once defended the country from enemy attack and was used as play equipment for children for about 30 years.

An express hauled by two steam locomotives heads through The Square in 1911. In the 1950s a deviation was begun to remove the railway from the centre of the city. From 1959 some goods trains bypassed The Square using the Milson deviation, and from October 1963 all passenger trains used this route after a new station was opened on the deviation. Freight trains ceased using the central city goods yards in May 1965.

Merle Sneddon collection

Graham Stewart collection

Graham Radcliffe collection

Graham Stewart

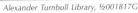

Alexander Turnbull Library, ½001817G

Graham Stewart

Bulls, the southern gateway to the Rangitikei, at the junction of State Highway One and State Highway Three, was first called Bull Town after English woodcarver James Bull who had designed panelling in the British House of Commons at Westminster before settling in New Zealand. James Bull established the first hotel and store in the village. 150 km north of Wellington, the settlement has a quaint cluster of shops selling antiques, bric-a-brac and crafts and is a popular stopping place for motorists.

In September 1950 the City of Wanganui held a carnival weekend before the tramway services closed. A 1891 Baldwin steam tram with the nickname of 'Puffing Billy', used in the construction of the Gonville and Castlecliff line in 1911-1912 and during a major power failure for three months in 1920, was brought out of storage after it had lain dormant for 30 years and used with old tram trailers to give children rides up and down Victoria Avenue. The electric tram in the foreground was about to leave for Castlecliff. The trams ran to the suburbs of Aramoho, Wanganui East, Gonville and Castlecliff. A private company, Greyhound Buses Limited, took over from the trams.

Graham Stewart

Graham Stewart collection

The Avenue from the Bridge. Wanganui. F.G.R 732.

Wanganui, founded in 1841, was one of the New Zealand Company's earliest settlements; Maori occupation of the area dates way back to about 1350. Situated on the banks of the Whanganui River, it became a bustling provincial centre when coastal shipping was the only way to move cargo in and out of town. The town was first called Petre after a New Zealand Company director, the name being changed to Wanganui in 1844. The Anglican-established Wanganui Collegiate School was founded here in 1854.

Above: Looking from the city bridge (1871) up Victoria Avenue shortly after the trams started running in 1908. The original two-lane bridge was replaced with a four-lane bridge and two arches in 1970.

Graham Stewart

John M. Bettle collection

Graham Stewart collection

In Wanganui, like many cities and towns around the country, the post office was the most architecturally impressive building in the community where townsfolk would meet. The Wanganui post office's clock tower (built 1902), at the Victoria Avenue junction with Ridgeway Street, suffered the same fate as others when it was removed as it was classified an earthquake risk. The Watt Memorial now stands in the centre of the street.

The Dublin Street bridge, a structure that took two years and seven months to build and gave the suburb of Wanganui East a direct road link, was opened in November 1914. After the customary cutting of the ribbon at the official opening by the mayor, T.B. Williams, the first vehicle to trundle across the bridge was an electric tram.

Graham Stewart

The Whanganui River flows from its source on Mount Tongariro, winding through North Island heartland, the Whanganui National Park and the city of Wanganui to the Tasman Sea. From the days of being an important Maori canoe route to the European steam-driven riverboats, it is an historic waterway.

Two riverboats, PS *Waimarie* (1900) and MV *Wairua* (1904), have been restored and again operate on the river for tourists.

Left: The PS *Waimarie* on its maiden voyage in 1900 with not a woman in sight! The *Waimarie* was launched as the *Aotea* and renamed the *Waimarie* when purchased by Hatrick and Company in 1902.

Below: Today the PS *Waimarie*, built at Poplar, London, and transported in kitset form to Wanganui, is New Zealand's last operating paddle steamer. For almost 50 years the PS *Waimarie* plied the river to Pipiriki, navigating the rapids and carrying cargo, mail, river dwellers and tourists.

Whanganui Riverboat Centre collection

Graham Stewart

Alexander Turnbull Library, ½006028G

Alexander Turnbull Library, ½07770G

Hawera, the principal town on the plains of South Taranaki, surveyed in 1866, suffered a series of fires. The first occurred in July 1884 when a hotel was razed, then five business premises were destroyed in August 1895, and in 1912 a large proportion of the main street was razed. This all seemed rather spooky as the Maori meaning of Hawera is 'the burnt place' or 'breath of fire'. After the devastating 1912 fire, a water tower was built to solve the poor water pressure problem and to make fire-fighting easier. The heritage landmark is lit at night and can be climbed (215 steps) for a great view. An earthquake within months of the tower opening in January 1914 caused it to list toward the south, but as the tanks were filled, the lean was rectified by engineers. It still has a slight lean of 75 mm.

Above right: Hotel verandahs and hotel fire escapes made good grandstands to watch a parade pass through town at the height of the 1930s depression. The White Hart Hotel on the corner (right) still stands. It was originally named the Empire, was burnt down in 1884 and rebuilt soon after. In the great fire of 1895, it was scorched but not burnt. During the 1920s it was remodelled with verandahs added to its façade and was renamed the White Hart Hotel. The building (right foreground) is a classical style of architecture, built in 1926, and is still the branch office of the National Bank of New Zealand.

Graham Stewart

Taranaki

Mount Egmont, North Island, New Zealand.

Graham Stewart collection

NEW YEAR

I wish you +
all the wealth
that lies + +
within the + +
New Year's heart,

MOUNT EGMONT, N.Z.

Copyright.   Tanner Bros., Ltd   X 51—225

Graham Stewart

The cone-shaped volcano of Mount Taranaki (Mount Egmont), 2518 metres in height, watches over this pastoral heartland. Taranaki is home to New Zealand's energy production of onshore and offshore natural gas and oil fields. The Egmont National Park (33,500 hectares) containing Mount Taranaki/Egmont was formed in 1900 and is the second oldest national park. The mountain last erupted in 1775 and the present cone, formed some 20,000 years ago, is considered dormant.

Merle Sneddon collection

Eltham was named after a town in Kent, England, and was first settled in the 1870s. In July 1883 it was gazetted as Eltham Village Settlement.

Left: Standing on the horizon near the top of Bridge Street is the Coronation Hotel (on the right), which was named after King Edward VII in the year of his coronation, 1902. The hotel was used as a set during the filming of the 1984 film *Came a Hot Sunday* which starred New Zealand comedian Billy T. James.

Eltham is known for industrial firsts: Chinese businessman Chew Chong exported the first butter to England in 1884; the first dairy factory was built here in 1887; and in 1906 Bridge and High Streets became the first tar macadam-surfaced streets in New Zealand. The town has had a tradition of cheese-making which continues today.

Graham Stewart

Below: Stratford is nestled beneath the slopes of Mount Taranaki and was named after Shakespeare's birthplace. It was first named Stratford-upon-Patea and many of its streets are named after the Bard's characters. As a European settlement, the town was surveyed on the banks of the Patea River in 1877 and by 1897 was a bustling centre. In the 1920s it was the first place in the southern hemisphere to screen a 'talking picture' at the TET Kings Theatre. The glockenspiel clock tower (*below right*) on Broadway has a unique Shakespearean theme with Romeo and Juliet emerging at 10 am, 1 pm, 3 pm, daily. The original clock faces from the old post office tower of 1924 were used again when this tower was constructed in 1998.

Below left: Traffic roundabouts on Broadway mean traffic no longer has to slow down to go around corners at 8 miles an hour as was the regulation in 1918 when the town celebrated the end of the First World War with a peace parade down Broadway.

Alexander Turnbull Library, 1/1 007922G

Graham Stewart

Alexander Turnbull Library, ½001074G

Graham Stewart

Opunake on Surf Highway 45 is a South Taranaki settlement which started life like many others as an isolated place with access mainly by sea until the late 1880s. The first wharf of 1891 was felled by stormy seas and was replaced by a second wharf which closed in the 1920s, as heavy seas often made berthing a problem.

Above: Middleton's Hotel on Tasman Street, when E. O'Meara was the licensee, was a popular stopping place for thirsty motorists c1912. The hotel changed its name to the Club Hotel and still offers the same warm hospitality.

Graham Stewart

Right: On the main street is a bronze statue of Sir Peter Snell which was modelled by Dr Fridtjof Hanson, bronzed by Ross Wilson and commissioned by the Egmont Community Arts Council in May 2007. Peter Snell was born in Opunake in 1938. He was the winner of three Olympic gold medals for 800 and 1500 metres and two Commonwealth Games gold medals for the mile and 880 yards track events in the 1960s. He set seven individual world records during his athletic career, including twice setting a new mark for the mile distance.

DEVON ST. NEW PLYMOUTH. N.Z. A3659. ALDERSLEY

Graham Stewart collection

New Plymouth, the urban heart of the province, is the servicing centre for the farming and the $2 billion energy industries in the district. The artificial harbour is the west coast's only international deep-water port.

When traders and whalers arrived in the 1820s, the city started to grow. In 1841 Plymouth Company ships brought British migrants to settle, and within a few years there were thousands of new arrivals. The first Plymouth Company ship, *William Bryan,* landed 148 settlers on 31 March 1841. In 1885 co-operative dairy factories opened in Opunake and Inglewood.

Historically, Maori fought over Taranaki for centuries and again in the 1820s when Waikato tribes successfully invaded. When the local Te Atiawa tribe returned, having fled to the Cook Strait region, they found the invaders had sold land to English immigrant settlers. This led to the Taranaki Land Wars of the 1860s against the government.

Graham Stewart

Graham Stewart

Merle Sneddon collection

Graham Stewart

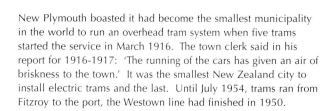

Graham Stewart

New Plymouth boasted it had become the smallest municipality in the world to run an overhead tram system when five trams started the service in March 1916. The town clerk said in his report for 1916-1917: 'The running of the cars has given an air of briskness to the town.' It was the smallest New Zealand city to install electric trams and the last. Until July 1954, trams ran from Fitzroy to the port, the Westown line had finished in 1950.

Facing page: Looking south down Devon Street shortly after the electric trams started running in 1916.
Above left: A trolley-bus from Westown turns into Robe Street in front of the old post office (1906). New Plymouth was the only provincial centre to operate a trolley-bus system. The service replaced the Westown tram route in October 1950 and ran for 17 years until October 1967.
Above: The junction of Devon and Egmont Streets was an important intersection in the days of trams.
Left: Following the demolition of the old post office, together with the town's landmark tower, public response saw the much loved tower reincarnated in a replica structure in 1985 and the original clock faces installed to once again give out the time around town.

Recreation Grounds, New Plymouth, N. Z.   Copyright No. 119

This view from above the band rotunda overlooking Poet's Bridge over Pukekura Park's main lake has changed little over the last century. The hand-coloured printed postcard above was issued in the early years of the 20th century.

The postcard below, issued at about the same time, shows Mount Taranaki/Egmont as the dramatic backdrop – the perfect picture postcard for tourists to cherish with the snow-covered mountain rising majestically in the centre. It was not until the author visited Pukekura Park to obtain a matching photograph that he discovered the postcards of the past, featuring the mountain, were fakes! The mountain can only be seen from the tea kiosk.

F. T. Series. No. 38. Recreation Ground, New Plymouth, and Mount Egmont.

Graham Stewart

Pukekura Park in New Plymouth is one of the finest botanical landscape parks in the country, covering 45 hectares, with Brooklands Park and the Bowl of Brookland, an outdoor sound-shell nearby. Its fine trees, lawns, fernery, rhododendrons, waterfalls, lakes and streams connected by shady paths, take visitors to a nature world only minutes from the city centre. The formal opening of the Recreation Grounds (original name) was in May 1876, the main lake being formed in 1878 and Poet's Bridge opening on 11 March 1884. A tragic postscript was that the donor of the bridge, Mr J.T. Davis, was found drowned under the bridge in 1891. The park was renamed Pukekura Park in 1902.

Right: From the Pukekura Park tea kiosk, a perfect view of Mount Taranaki/Egmont.

Graham Stewart

Graham Stewart

State Highway 43, known as the Forgotten World Highway, runs between Stratford and Taumarunui, a distance of 155 km through sub-tropical rain forests, saddles and valleys and a hand-dug tunnel.

At Whangamomona, 76 km from Stratford, a village settled in 'The Valley of Plenty' in 1895, is the Whangamomona Hotel which is like the Rovers Return in television's Coronation Street where all the locals gather. An Edwardian pub built in 1902, it was burnt to the ground in 1910 and rebuilt the following year; in 2005 the hotel was awarded 'Best Country Hotel'.

Facing Page: A muddy, memorable occasion was the visit in 1903 of the Premier, the Rt Hon Richard Seddon and his entourage to Whangamomona.

Graham Stewart

Graham Stewart

In 1988 when regional government announced the moving of provincial boundaries, that this Taranaki village would in future be part of the Manawatu region, the locals protested and declared themselves a republic! They had always represented Taranaki at rugby and would never change. Republican Day is now celebrated biennially in January when the double-digit population swells to many thousands as people arrive by train, bus, car and on horseback to enjoy a pint of Whanga ale and partake in the gumboot-throwing, sheep races, whip-cracking, possum-skinning, wood-chopping and the presidential elections.

Left: The border guard, a full frontal outside toilet.

New Zealand Memories collection

John de Bonnaire, courtesy New Zealand Memories

Graham Stewart

The Moki tunnel, built in 1936 on the Forgotten World Highway north of Whangamomona, is a one-way, 180-metre-long, spooky earth tunnel. The floor was lowered in 1985 to enable large cattle trucks passage. The black-and-white photographs were taken in 1961.

New Zealand Memories collection

Early roads around New Zealand were always a nightmare when it rained and during the winter months in the days before tarseal surfaced roads. This classic photograph from the 1920s shows the driver, leaning on his two-door, canvas-topped car with running boards, looking casually at Mount Taranaki (Mount Egmont in those days).

Graham Stewart

Alexander Turnbull Library, ½040280F

Lake Waikaremoana, a 54 square kilometre expanse of water, is in Te Urewera National Park (212,672 hectares), the North Island's largest untouched native forest. It is the home of the Tuhoe tribe, a land of myths. The lake is surrounded by abrupt forest-covered mountains of kahikatea, northern rata, rimu, totara and tawa on the lower ground, and high above red and silver beech. It is a retreat for native birds: kaka, kiwi, kokako, morepork, pigeon (kereru), tui, shining and long-tailed cuckoo all inhabit this park.

Above: Guests admire the magnificent view over the lake to the west arm when the Lake House Hotel stood on Whaitiri Point. This 15-room accommodation block was opened in 1903, and when trout were released in the lake in 1908, the hotel was enlarged. Electricity was installed in 1926 and the lounge and dining areas were upgraded in 1933. In 1936 all bedrooms were fitted with hot and cold running water. The 1950s were the golden years with the hotel becoming a licensed tourist hotel with international chefs, a games and billiard room, dance floor and weekly cinemas. Trips on the lake on the launch *Ruapani* were part of the service. The economic downturns of the 1970s saw the hotel close in 1972 and eventually demolished.

Graham Stewart

Hawke's Bay

New Zealand Herald

Alan Bellamy collection

The first Wairoa bridge, built in 1888, was severely damaged in the 1931 earthquake. 15 months later a pontoon ferry (*above*) started a service across the river. The second bridge, opened in 1933, was destroyed by Cyclone Bola on 8 March 1988. The present bridge was opened on 7 February 1990 by Queen Elizabeth II.

The Mohaka rail viaduct (built in 1937) between Kotemaori and Waihua, is a monument to early New Zealand engineering and is the highest in the land at 97 metres. Railcar Rm 32 stops for a photograph on the viaduct in 1939.

Graham Stewart

TARAWERA SADDLE NAPIER-TAUPO RD.

Alexander Turnbull Library, ¼019629F

The original hotel on this site, named the Tarawera Hot Springs Hotel, was part of the folklore of the old Taupo Road in the days when horse-drawn coaches would stop so their passengers could have a drink and a bite to eat. Fire flattened the old two-storey wooden pub in 1965, in the days when a liquor licence would be revoked if the publican did not resume serving alcohol within 24 hours. The locals made sure the beer flowed the next night, using a surviving shed and a mini-beer tanker within the prescribed time! The replacement building is a Lockwood structure (*below*) and today trades as the Tarawera Tavern.

Graham Stewart

Alexander Turnbull Library, MNZ0711 ¼F

The original Rangitaiki Hotel was built as an Armed Constabulary canteen at Opepe. When the township faded, the building was bought and moved by the coaching company of Crowther and McAuley to the inhospitable pumice desert land of the Rangitaiki Plains. Here, south-bound stagecoach travellers would overnight before proceeding on to Napier. Beer still flows from the hotel building of today; only the petrol pumps are dry.

Graham Stewart

Alexander Turnbull Library, 8792 01/2

The streets of Napier were designed in the 1850s by politician and poet Alfred Domett who gave the city's streets a literary flavour with such names as Browning, Byron, Burns, Chaucer, Dickens, Milton, Shakespeare and Tennyson; and a scientific tone with Carlyle, Emerson and Faraday.

Above: Looking down Tennyson Street from the Marine Parade in 1909 with the ornate band rotunda (1894) of wrought-iron tracery and slender fluted pillars in the foreground and the Masonic Hotel (1897) with its elaborate verandah balustrades in the early years of the 20th century. All was flattened in the 1931 earthquake. The first hotel on this site was a wooden building built in 1861 and burnt to the ground in 1896.

Graham Stewart

Hastings Street, Napier N Z

Graham Stewart collection

Left: Hastings Street has had two lives like all the inner streets of Napier. The first Criterion Hotel on the left, a wooden colonial building with a verandah surround facing Hastings Street, disappeared in flames in 1931 along with the rest of the street and was replaced with a new building with a Spanish façade. The two-storey wooden Clarendon Hotel facing Hastings Street, in the distance at the foot of Shakespeare Road, survived the fire of 1931 but finally succumbed to fire in the early 1960s.

These three views of Hastings Street were taken c1900s, c1920s and 2007.

Hasting Street. Napier. F.G.R.4843.

Merle Sneddon collection

Maori, like Europeans, found the Hawke's Bay a fruit bowl for harvesting and a climate ideal for a good life. Cook passed by in October 1769 and the French visited the bay in 1827. Whalers made Ahuriri a depot and a trading place in the 1830s, and William Colenso founded the Waitangi mission station by the Ngaruroro River near Clive in 1844.

During the land wars of the 1860s a group of Hauhau marched on Napier in 1866 but were repulsed at Omarunui; another band of Hauhau was defeated near Eskdale. Te Ngati Kahungunu of Hawke's Bay were on the whole sympathetic to the British. In 1858 Napier became the provincial capital of Hawke's Bay. The country's oldest winery was established in 1865 at The Mission vineyards at Greenmeadows.

Graham Stewart

This wooden Victorian town was replaced after the earthquake and fire with the fashionable architecture vogue of the 1930s, the modern American style of the era which is known today as Art Deco. In February each year Napier hosts an Art Deco weekend of the 1930s with wine, food, jazz, dancing, vintage cars, plane rides and a variety of entertainment. Napier has one of the most outstanding collections of Art Deco buildings in the world.

Hastings St. Napier. N.Z. F.G.R. 7503.

3 February 1931 was typical of Hawke's Bay in the summer – the day was warm with a clear sky and hardly a breath of wind to stir the dust, when at 10.46 am Hawke's Bay was hit by an earthquake with a magnitude of 7.9 on the Richter scale and an epicentre onshore near Bay View. Fatalities numbered 258; this was New Zealand's worst natural disaster. Within four minutes fire broke out in the commercial centre of Napier which left the city a blackened ruin. The earthquake uplifted more than 3000 hectares of seabed where modern suburbs are today and gave Hawke's Bay land for the airport.

Looking south along Hastings Street from the junction of Emerson Street over the years.
Above: Waiting for a tram in 1921.
Facing page:
Top: The deserted street after the 1931 earthquake.
Lower: Today it is once again a bustling commercial centre.

Hastings St Napier

Lovell-Smith collection

Sailors pick their way through rubble covering Tennyson Street outside the remains of the Masonic Hotel on the left. HMS *Veronica* was in port when the earthquake struck on 3 February 1931 and her sailors began rescue work immediately. When the news reached Auckland, both HMS *Diomede* and HMS *Dunedin* sailed at full speed (averaging 24 knots down the coast), carrying doctors, nurses and first-aid stores. They arrived in Hawke Bay at 8.30 the next morning.

Graham Stewart

Lovell-Smith collection

The Hawke's Bay earthquake of 3 February 1931 flattened the central business district of Napier. The Public Trust building on the corner of Dalton and Tennyson Streets, looked like St Paul's Cathedral in London during the blitz of the Second World War, standing alone surrounded by 'a hell's delight of broken masonry, crushed cars and mangled cycles'. It was one of the few buildings to survive intact in downtown Napier.

Graham Stewart

Graham Stewart

The bronze statue of 'Pania of the Reef' on the Marine Parade was based on Maori folklore. 'Pania, lured by the siren voice of the sea people, swam out to meet them. When she endeavoured to return to her lover she was transformed into the reef which now lies beyond the Napier Breakwater.' The statue was a gift of the Napier Thirty Thousand Club and was unveiled by Prime Minister the Rt Hon Sidney Holland in June 1954.

An Italian sculptor made the statue, using a photograph of May Robin, a pupil of Hukarere Maori Girls' College, as a model for Pania's head.

Above left: May Robin was photographed by the statue on the day it was unveiled by the prime minister.

"Pania" Statue. Marine Parade, Napier, N.Z. 7795. A.B Hurst & Son Photo.

Graham Stewart collection

A pre-earthquake view of a Napier city-bound blue and cream tram in Shakespeare Road, picking up a passenger by France Road. The Napier Girls' High School is on the horizon. The school buildings and the trams did not survive the earthquake. 3 February happened to have been the first day of the new school year in 1931.

Port Ahuriri was Napier's main port until 1931. The Iron Pot, as it was once called, was a busy haven for shipping before the earthquake lifted the seabed and drained water from the basin. In the distance can be seen the North British Freezing Works which ended in ruins when the quake hit. Dredging has since made the basin a haven again, this time for pleasure craft.

Graham Stewart

The name of Watties is synonymous with this city. Sir James Wattie (1902-1974) built the industrial giant J. Wattie Canneries Limited through his leadership, energy, courage and skill to show the way. He never lost the common touch: he knew the staff of the Hastings factory mostly by first names and he could do most of the jobs, having learnt the hard way. He built an industry that transformed the economies of the Heretaunga Plains and the Poverty Bay flats.

On Monday, 19 February 1962, when the Hastings factory was at near peak production, fire broke out and quickly raced out of control, destroying the factory except the boilers, the fruit and vegetable canning machinery and the can-making plant. It was James Wattie himself who rolled up his sleeves and directed the task of tidying up and restoring production which he had rolling again within 50 hours of the disaster.

Left: James Wattie watches with a staff member as the factory collapses into a pile of ashes.

Alexander Turnbull Library, 1/1 002997F

Lovell-Smith collection

The Albert Hotel has stood on Heretaunga Street since horse and coach days and survived the 1931 earthquake by being on the right side of the street at the time. Fire gutted the block diagonally opposite and the Grand Hotel on the corner of Russell Street.

Above right: As workmen tackle clearing rubble from Heretaunga Street following the 1931 quake, the Albert Hotel can be seen standing tall down the street on the corner of Karamu Road with its name clearly showing.

Graham Stewart collection

Hastings began when early settlers purchased 7000 hectares of swampland from Maori in 1864 and developed the town; as the community prospered, the harvesting of fruit grew, to be followed by viticulture. Hastings, like Napier, suffered destruction in the 1931 Hawke's Bay earthquake with 88 people killed. Only 20 km from Napier, the city is on the fertile fruit and wine-producing Heretaunga Plains. Food processing and the export of tinned and frozen food to all parts of the world are big business in Hastings and the surrounding area.

Above and below: The railroad has been running through the middle of the town since 1874, crossing Heretaunga Street, the main street, by the city's clock tower. On the corner of Russell Street is the post-earthquake Spanish mission-style Westermans building of 1932 (below centre), designed by Edmund Anscombe and Associates. Within the Hastings clock tower (1934) hang the former post office bells that fell with the old post office tower (1909) on to Queen Street during the earthquake.

Graham Stewart

The Hastings Municipal Theatre (left), designed by Henry Eli White (1914), and the Municipal Building (opened 1917), since vacated by the council, was designed by Albert Garnett. These buildings on the corner of Hastings and Heretaunga Streets are the city's most splendid architecturally with their Spanish mission-style façade.

Alexander Turnbull Library, ½046112G

Havelock North has a very English village atmosphere and is the home of two English-style private girls' boarding schools. Towering over the village is Te Mata Peak, only 6 km up a winding road to the summit of 399 metres, from where there are expansive views of Hawke's Bay and beyond, even Mt Ruapehu, on a clear day.

The Transformer House (centre), designed by James Chapman-Taylor in 1915, is still the centrepiece of the village and now houses the visitor information centre. Chapman-Taylor designed the small building where five roads meet so that it would look the same from all angles, with no obvious front or back. It was originally built to house the power transformer when electricity arrived in the area. The building was later altered and used as a bus shelter, and in 1937 a bracket clock was purchased from the Hastings City Council which replaced the Chapman-Taylor bell tower.

Graham Stewart

Alexander Turnbull Library,G45823½

Simon Crawford collection

Waipukurau, 53 km south-west of Hastings and known locally as 'Wai-puk', is only 8 km south of Waipawa. Both are farming centres in southern Hawke's Bay. During the Second World War groups of American servicemen would make trips to 'Wai-puk' just to be photographed by the town sign, as they considered the name equal to visiting 'Timbuktu' or 'Whykickamoocow'.

Above: High Street, Waipawa, 1927.   *Above*: Ruataniwha Street, Waipukurau, c1915.

Graham Stewart

12 km north of Waipukurau is Te Aute College at Pukehou. It was founded as an Anglican mission school for young Maori. Former pupils include distinguished Maori leaders Sir Apirana Ngata, Sir Maui Pomare and Sir Peter Buck.

Sir Apirana Ngata was the first Maori to graduate from a New Zealand University with a BA in 1893, an MA in 1894 and an LL.B in 1896 and subsequently an honorary doctorate. He was MP for Eastern Maori from 1905 to 1943 for Liberal, United and National. He was knighted in 1927. From 1928 to 1934 he was Minister of Native Affairs and the Cook Islands.

Sir Maui Pomare, born in 1876, left Te Aute in 1892 and was the first Maori doctor. He became an MP for Western Maori and held the portfolios of Health, Internal Affairs and Minister-in-charge of the Cook Islands in the Reform government of 1912 to 1928. He was knighted in 1922 and died in 1930.

Sir Peter Buck left Te Aute in 1898 and graduated from Otago University in medicine in 1904. He was MP for Northern Maori and sat briefly in cabinet as a minister representing the native race. He later became director and a professor of anthropology at Yale University.

Archives New Zealand, AAQT 6539 A377

Out from Waipukurau, 8 km south-west of Porangahau on a small ridge, is one of the longest place names in the world. Locals refer to the hill simply as Taumata, but its full name will continue to challenge the Welsh town of Llanfairpwllgwngyllgogerychwyrn-drobwllllantysiliogogogoch which also claims the record. The Maori translation of the New Zealand name is: 'the hill on which Tamatea, the chief of great physical stature and renown, played a lament on his flute to the memory of his brother'.

Graham Stewart

Graham Stewart

Dannevirke and Norsewood were settled by Danish and Norwegian migrants in the 1870s who arrived on the ships *Ballarat* and *Hovding* and cleared a dense virgin totara forest to build their towns and farm the district. They had been warned the land was bush country without any open land and only those who were sober, industrious, of good moral character, of sound mind and in good health, need apply.

Above: All that remains of the grand Victorian railway station, c1920s, is the corrugated-iron canopy with the end cast-iron New Zealand Railways standard decorative infill and the rose garden.

Above: The old Masonic Hotel on the corner of Barraud Street and High Street, Dannevirke, when S.L. Parsons was the licensee, has since been trimmed in height but is still a dignified building of the period. High Street is now one continual convoy of traffic.

The Wairarapa

Merle Sneddon collection

Merle Sneddon collection

Woodville is located at the junction of State Highways Two and Three, with the Tararua and Ruahine Ranges to the west and the Puketoi and Waepapa mountains to the east. It is the gateway to Hawke's Bay to the north, to the Wairarapa to the south and to the Manawatu to the west. On the north side of the Manawatu Gorge is the Te Apiti wind farm. 10 km south at Mangatainoka is the home of the Tui Brewery, established in 1889 with its seven-storey tower.

Pahiatua (1881) was settled in an area then known as Forty Mile Bush in northern Wairarapa. The wide Main Street with gardens and trees down the centre on State Highway Two was planned for a railway line that never arrived in town. It was found more practicable to keep the railway line to the eastern bank of the Mangatainoka River. A camp during the Second World War held 'enemy aliens' moved from Somes Island in Wellington harbour. They were sent back to the island in 1944 when the camp became home for over 700 Polish children, refugees from war-torn Europe. Most became New Zealand citizens.

Graham Stewart

Eketahuna and Districts Early Settlers Museum

Eketahuna is between northern and southern Wairarapa and was once the southern boundary of the Forty Mile Bush. It was first named Mellemskov (in the middle of the forest) by government-assisted Scandinavian migrants who founded the town in 1872. The town has had many setbacks over the decades, including the great fire of 1908 and the earthquake of June 1942. The name 'Eketahuna' is used tongue-in-cheek to describe small-town New Zealand and is proudly quoted by locals.

Above: The main street with the Club Hotel (left), was put out of business by the 1942 earthquake and remained derelict until demolished many years later for the building of the new Commercial Hotel. On the right stand the Wairarapa Farmers Co-operative Association, the Bank of New Zealand and W. H. Wilson, coach builder and wheelwright on the corner of Main and Bridge Streets.

Graham Stewart

Wairarapa Archive collection

Masterton was founded by the Small Farms Association in 1854, led by Joseph Masters after whom the town was named. The concept of the association was to settle working people in villages and on the land. In the 1870s Masterton became the major commercial and distribution centre in the Wairarapa and a borough in 1877. The arrival of the railway from Wellington in 1880 heralded more growth. Masterton hosts the International Golden Shears competition in March each year.

Above: The 'Borough Bridge' where the stream through Robinson Park now runs. The post office tower is visible in the distance. The two bridges at the northern end of Queen Street were over separate arms of the Waipoua River.

Graham Stewart

Alexander Turnbull Library, ½089107F

Masterton's original post office was a single-level wooden building built in 1875 which was replaced by a building befitting the importance of the town when opened in May 1900. Those who voiced concern that the building was overly ornate were proven correct when masonry fell during an earthquake in 1904, killing a pedestrian. Citizens purchased a clock for the tower which was installed a few years after the official opening. The June 1942 earthquake badly damaged the tower which was later removed along with all the Victorian decoration. The third post office building (*below*) opened in 1962.

Above: Horse-drawn mail coaches prepare to depart.
Right: Looking south down Queen Street c1910.

Merle Sneddon collection

Graham Stewart

Muir and Moodie, Graham Stewart collection

Carterton, 14 km south-west of Masterton on State Highway Two, was first known as Three Mile Bush when settled in 1857. In 1859 the name was changed to Carterton after Charles Rooking Carter, who was an advocate of the Small Farms Association and a member of the Wellington provincial council. Alfred Booth, mayor from 1891 to 1902, started Carterton on the road to becoming the 'daffodil capital of the country' when he planted acres of bulbs in the paddocks around his homestead in the 1890s.

Above: Looking south along High Street, c1910, part of State Highway Two which runs through Carterton, with the corner of Broadway in the right foreground. Down High Street are the old Carterton post office and tower (1903); the clock and bells were installed in 1907. The tower, like many others around the country, was damaged by the 1942 earthquake and demolished.

Graham Stewart

Wairarapa Archive collection

Merle Sneddon collection

The now fashionable town of Greytown was the first planned inland town in New Zealand. It was another Wairarapa town settled by the Small Farms Association in 1854, a group of working-class men whose aim was to make it possible for men with little capital to purchase their own land. The town was named after Governor Sir George Grey (1812-1898). When settled, it was covered in dense bush which was rather ironic as it was the first New Zealand town to celebrate Arbour Day on 3 July 1890. Dignitaries, Greytown School pupils and residents planted 153 native trees, 12 of which have survived.

Above: The Council Chambers (left) on Main Street, Greytown, c1905, with Fred Muir's variety store next door and, further along the street, Arthur Jones' bakery.

Featherston was surveyed in 1856 with the first auction of sections held the following year. Growth was slow until the opening of the railway from Wellington in 1878. During the First World War a military camp was built just north of the town to accommodate approximately 8000 men. During the Second World War the camp was used as a Japanese prisoner-of-war camp. The camp was finally used by the men who built the Rimutaka railway tunnel in the early 1950s. 63 km north-east from Wellington, Featherston is at the foot of the Rimutaka Range.

Above: Looking south toward the Fitzgerald and Revans Streets junction in October 1912. The Royal Hotel was built in 1869, burnt to the ground in 1893 and rebuilt.

Graham Stewart

Merle Sneddon collection

Martinborough started life as Waihenga or Wharekaka in 1870, and then in 1879 along came wealthy run holder John Martin who purchased land and founded a new town, giving it his own name. He subdivided 600 urban sections and laid the town out in the shape of the Union Jack. Few streets have been added since although there was a planned subdivision off New York Street in the 1900s, with a block of streets bearing the names of native trees, which didn't proceed. John Martin named the streets after favourite cities he had visited, prominent people and memorable streets. The village of Martinborough has flourished to become the wine capital of the region since grapes for wine production were planted in the late 1970s. Since 1992 an annual wine and food festival, Toast Martinborough, brings thousands to the township. The town is now surrounded by vineyards, olive groves and rolling farmland.

Above: Looking from the town square down Kitchener Street to the Martinborough Hotel (c1900s left) and the post office (1896) on the other side of the road. The hotel was refurbished in early 1996 and once again is a quality country inn.

Graham Stewart

Early motorists found the Rimutaka hill road was not for the fainthearted with its tortuous narrow bends and no fences to give them some feeling of security from falling hundreds of metres into the valley below. It was a journey that required both driving skills and careful navigation. The road was not fenced until the 1920s.

Above: There was time for a photograph before the hill – a group of motorists takes time out south of Featherston on the Wairarapa side of the Rimutaka Ranges before tackling the hill c1916.

Above: A motorist c1916 poses for a photographer at the summit of the Rimutaka hill road, with his passengers dressed appropriately for open-air travel standing by the car.

Graham Stewart

William Main collection

For 77 years, from October 1878 to October 1955, Wellington-bound trains laboured up the Rimutaka Incline at six miles an hour, as they traversed the mountain range dividing the Wairarapa from the Hutt Valley. The incline, some 4.8 km long, climbed 265 metres on a gradient of 1 in 15, around many curves of 17 degrees, in some places as steep as 1 in 13. Trains were hauled by locomotives equipped with horizontal wheels that gripped each side of a double-headed centre rail which was laid sideways on pedestals placed between the running rails. The horizontal driving wheels were brought to bear against each face of the centre rail by means of powerful springs. Special brakes were applied to the central rail when running downhill at 10 miles an hour to keep the speed in check. The special locomotives, known as Fell after John Barraclough Fell who patented the concept in 1863, could each haul 65 tonnes. The maximum allowable load of any one freight train could not exceed 260 tonnes which meant four locomotives had to be spaced throughout the train so that each engine could handle its individual weight allowance. The six Fell engines were classified as H class and the first four were named: H1 *Mt Cenis*, H2 *Mt Cook*, H3 *Mt Egmont* and H4 *Mt Tongariro*. In September 1880 two carriages were blown off the rails by gale-force winds, resulting in three children being killed and 21 passengers injured. This occurred as it rounded a 100-metre-radius curve on an open embankment spanning a gully known as Siberia, 1200 metres from the Summit, when a gust estimated at just under 200 km an hour struck the train. This rugged rail route with atrocious winds and weather became redundant in 1955 when the Rimutaka railway tunnel (8.79 km) was opened. Today the original railway route is the Rimutaka Rail Trail which runs for 17 km from Kaitoke in the west to Cross Creek, south of Featherston, in the east.

Rimutaka Incline N.Z. 4032. F.G.R.

Simon Crawford collection

Graham Stewart collection

Alexander Turnbull Library, ½028142F

Levin is today the largest town in the Horowhenua district, 95 km north of Wellington on State Highway One. It was not until the 1880s that the Muaupoko tribe was prepared to sell land for the township, making it a late starter in the district for Europeans to settle. Only when the railway opened in 1886 did the town start to grow. The town was named after a director of the Wellington and Manawatu Railway Company, W.H. Levin. 21 km to the south is Otaki where the Ngati Toa chief Te Rauparaha made his mainland base.

Above: The three-storey Hotel Arcadia on Oxford Street would have been a mighty tall building in the days when this photograph was taken.

The steam-hauled Wellington mail train pulls out of Paekakariki in 1915, the old railway town immortalised in song. The settlement is part of railway folklore, remembered for the old New Zealand Railways 'Paekok Pie' when the refreshment rooms did a brisk trade as steam locomotives were changed for electrics, until 1967.

It is still an important railway town where diesel and electric trains pass through. It is also home to one of the major active steam locomotive museums in the country.

Graham Stewart

Wellington Region
and the
Hutt Valley

Te Whanga Nui a Tara, the first name given to the Wellington area, was where Whatonga's people came from Hawke's Bay to settle and founded the Ngati Tara tribe. The New Zealand Company's ship *Aurora* arrived in the harbour on 22 January 1840, bringing the first European settlers, in the days when the curves of Lambton Quay were the beach front. William Wakefield had arrived on the *Tory* in September 1839 to negotiate the purchase of land from Maori.

Alexander Turnbull Library, F146498 ½

A.H. & A.W. Reed postcard, Graham Stewart collection

Although the Ngauranga Gorge road had been straightened over the years, it was still a narrow and difficult road in the 1930s. With the predicted influx of traffic to the Centennial Exhibition at Rongotai in 1940, the road was closed in August 1938 for realigning and widening. All vehicles were diverted via the Ngaio Gorge or Onslow Road during the closure. The road reopened with ceremony on 4 November 1939. In later years the gorge road has been widened to six lanes.

The cable cars first climbed the hill to Kelburn in February 1902. The original trams ran for 76 years and made their last trips on Friday, 22 September 1978. Just over a year later, on 20 October 1979, the present-day Swiss system with chalet-style stations opened.

At the top of the line in the old winding house, the Wellington Cable Car Museum houses restored examples of the first cable cars and trailers. The museum opened in December 2000.

Graham Stewart

Alexander Turnbull Library, G25577 1/1

The small commercial centre of Lower Hutt, when the population was about 1500 and St James Anglican Church stood tall c1880s. This was the second church building, opened in March 1880 and destroyed by fire in June 1946. The bridge in the photograph is the fourth bridge to span the river. Built of totara in 1872, it was a toll bridge until January 1897 and lasted until replaced by the fifth bridge in 1904. The first bridge had been built in 1844, the second in 1847, the third in 1856. The sixth bridge, named after Councillor D.A. Ewen, was opened by Sir Joseph Ward in March 1929. Today's bridge (*right*) was opened in 1979, being the seventh to span the river at the entrance to Hutt City.

Graham Stewart

Petone, at the southern end of the Hutt Valley facing Wellington Harbour, was the first attempt at colonisation by the New Zealand Company, brief as the settlement was at Pito-one (the end of the sand beach), now known as Petone. The paramount Te Ati Awa chief sold a large tract of land around the harbour to the New Zealand Company. In a short time flooding led many settlers to leave for the new site at Thorndon. Those who remained had to handle regular floods until stopbanks were completed in 1900.

G Salmon

Three months before disaster struck – it is January 1968 – the inter-island ferry *Wahine* has just turned to port and is about to go astern and berth at the inter-island wharf. The time is a few minutes before 7 am. The photographer has captured an early-morning chapter of Wellington's history.

Museum of Wellington City and Sea

On 10 April 1968 tropical cyclone Giselle struck New Zealand. During the storm the *Wahine* became a victim, going out of control and striking Barrett Reef at the entrance to the harbour. With loss of power, the *Wahine* drifted up-harbour and foundered approximately 400 metres off the Seatoun foreshore by Steeple Beacon with the loss of 51 lives.

Right: The New Zealand shipping Company's SS *Ruapehu* leaves Queens Wharf under steam c1887. Sails were used to conserve coal at sea.

In the early days people and produce all arrived by sea.
Today Wellington is a container port and hosts an armada of super cruise ships in the summer months.

Below: Cunard liner *Queen Victoria* leaves Wellington on a round-the-world maiden voyage in February 2008, while the suburbs of Oriental Bay and Mount Victoria bask in the late afternoon sun.

Oil painting by W.W. Stewart

Graham Stewart

Connolly, William Main collection

Oriental Bay in the mid-1880s was starting to develop as a residential seaside haven close to the city. The railway line around the bay was built to take fill to the Te Aro reclamation scheme. Today, Oriental Bay is the Mediterranean of the south with people promenading from dawn to dusk, and cafés and restaurants with tables and chairs on the pavement. At night the water and the illuminated Norfolk pine trees reflect the ever-growing wall of high-rise apartment blocks. The beachfront has been a playground for Wellingtonians since before the sand was trucked in.

Graham Stewart

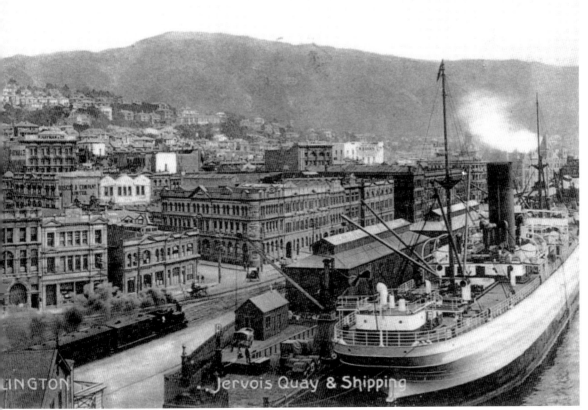

Jervois Quay & Shipping

Alistair Robb collection

Graham Stewart

Graham Stewart

Facing page top: Jervois Quay was where merchant warehouses were situated, when ships tied up across the road and steam-hauled trains ran along the quay to the Te Aro station at the corner of Wakefield and Tory Streets. The trains were joined by electric trams in December 1904. With the decline in coastal shipping more reclamation was undertaken in 1973 and the wharf sheds were demolished. Frank Kitts Park, created in 1990, is named after Wellington's longest serving mayor (1956-1974) and is now the venue for open-air concerts and gala events. The main mast from the inter-island ferry *Wahine* is a feature of the park promenade.

Above: In the right foreground is the Wellington Rowing Club building, erected in 1894 for the Wellington Naval Artillery Volunteers. Behind is the Star Boating Club's building of 1885 finally at rest, having moved several times to keep its position by the sea as harbour reclamation pushed the foreshore further out. In 1989 both clubhouses were moved and turned to face the city on the edge of a man-made lagoon as part of the harbour redevelopment.

Facing page left: When the Michael Fowler Centre opened in 1983, the plan was to demolish the old Town Hall but it was saved by public protest. The Town Hall has since been restored and is now part of Civic Square. Today, the City to Sea pedestrian bridge (right) over Jervois Quay links Frank Kitts Park with Civic Square.

Alexander Turnbull Library, F18017¼

Lambton Quay in the early 1950s showing the Midland Hotel (left foreground), Kirkcaldie and Stains department store (partially hidden) and the DIC building, now the Harbour City Centre. The buildings (right) on the sweep around the Quay have all gone except for Woodward House on the corner of Woodward Street (extreme right). Angle-parking certainly accommodated a lot of cars before trees replaced trams in the middle of the street.

New Zealand Herald

Graham Stewart

Cable Street in 1959 with a Chevrolet taxi the only movement, when the street was home for heavy industry, manufacturers and warehouses. The street now houses and displays the nation's treasures at the Museum of New Zealand Te Papa Tongarewa, which opened in February 1998. It is known as Te Papa which means Our Place.

Graham Stewart

Alexander Turnbull Library, F29400½

Looking up Willis Street c1861. The junction was known as Clay Point or Windy Point in the 1840s and 1850s and was later to be known as Stewart Dawson's Corner, where Willis Street, Lambton and Customhouse Quays meet. On the left is the original Empire Hotel, gutted by fire in 1876. The second Empire Hotel on this site was a three-storey building with a grand portico entrance which became an office block in 1955 until demolished in 1973. On the right is Miller's Commercial Inn and Tavern (large carriage lamp over the front door) where the Grand Hotel was built in 1906. Further up Willis Street are Izard and Bell solicitors and the *Evening Post*. Stewart Dawson's built the two-storey building in 1901 on the corner which still stands today (below right) and still has a jewellery shop fronting Lambton Quay.

John Plimmer (1812-1905), 'Father of Wellington', arrived Wellington 1841, carpenter, builder, brick manufacturer, land speculator, importer, merchant, landlord and politician. Instrumental in the extensive land reclamation of the Wellington waterfront and wharves, founding member of the Wellington Chamber of Commerce; Wellington Provincial Councillor, Wellington City Councillor. Founding director of the Wellington and Manawatu Railway Company. A bronze statue of John Plimmer and his dog Fritz is at the bottom of Plimmer's Steps off Lambton Quay.

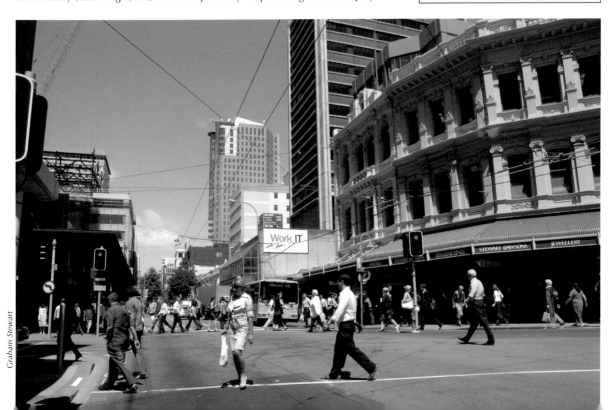

Graham Stewart

Alistair Robb collection

War Memorial, Wellington, N.Z.

The Cenotaph, built of white statuary marble and stone in 1929, is Wellington's War Memorial. It was dedicated to the fallen of the Great War in 1932 and rededicated in 1952 to include those who died in the Second World War.

On the hill behind (left), is the second Government House (built 1871) which became Parliament Buildings following the fire that destroyed the old debating chamber building in 1907, originally the Wellington Provincial Council Chambers. This wooden building remained when the new Parliament Buildings opened in the 1920s and was used for committee rooms and also housed the Parliamentary Ballroom until the executive wing of Parliament, nicknamed the Beehive (*below*) was built on this site in 1982. The northern wing (above right) and the dignified central colonnade, the entrance to Parliament Buildings, took nine years to build and opened in 1922. The facing of the building is South Island Takaka marble. The planned southern wing was never built on the site where the Beehive stands today.

Graham Stewart

William Main collection

There was only one horse and cart in sight when this photograph was taken of Courtenay Place in the 19th century. Today this part of Courtenay Place, with its many restaurants and cafés, moves at a racy pace day and night. The City Hotel in the distance is on the corner of Majoribanks Street and Kent Terrace. The building on this corner site was once a reincarnation of this old pub with the same name. From Majoribanks Street, Hawker Street winds up the hill to the left through open land.

Graham Stewart

The Right Reverend Sir Paul Reeves (1932 -   ), Wellington born, was the first Maori to head the Anglican church in New Zealand and the first Maori Governor-General (1985-1990). He was Bishop of Waiapu (1971-1979) and Bishop of Auckland (1979-1985).

William Main collection

Y.M.C.A. SWIMMING SPORTS 1.2.08. (START FOR THE 100 YDS. HDCP) ZAK PHOTO WGTON N.Z. 546.

The Te Aro salt-water baths on Oriental Parade were opened in January 1901 and used by Wellingtonians for over 60 years. When the baths were replaced with a covered complex in December 1963, they were named after a famous son of Wellington, Sir Bernard Freyberg. In the photograph above, taken at the Te Aro baths in February 1908, he is standing on the left. He would have turned 19 years of age the next month.

Sir Bernard Freyberg (1889-1963) emigrated to New Zealand with his parents when he was two years old and was educated at Wellington College. He won New Zealand swimming titles as a young man. He served with the British Army and commanded New Zealand troops in the Second World War. He was Governor-General of New Zealand (1946-1952). Elevated to the peerage in 1951, he took the title 'Baron Freyberg of Wellington, New Zealand, and Munstead, Surrey'.

Graham Stewart

Colin McDiarmid

Rugby was first played on Athletic Park (*above*) between Wellington and Christchurch teams on 6 April 1896. The first stand, built in 1898, could seat only 800. The Wellington Athletic Park Company had bought eight and a quarter acres in 1894, the assets of the company being sold to the Wellington Rugby Union in 1908. The first full-scale international rugby match by New Zealand at home – New Zealand v Great Britain – was played at Athletic Park, Wellington, on Saturday, 13 August 1904. New Zealand won the test 9 – 3. The final test at Athletic Park was against France on 26 June 1999. The score was the All Blacks 54, France 7.

Left: The new 35,000-seat cantilever-roofed, inner-city Westpac Stadium, where Aotea Quay meets Waterloo Quay, was officially opened on 3 January 2000 by the Governor-General Sir Michael Hardie Boys.

Colin McDiarmid

The birthplace of New Zealand's most famous short-story writer, Katherine Mansfield Beauchamp, is 25 Tinakori Road. Born on 14 October 1888, Katherine spent the first five years of her life here. The house has been restored by the Katherine Mansfield Birthplace Trust to the period of the Beauchamp family occupation (1888-1893), as shown in the lower plate, and is open to the public. Dr Truby King, founder of the Plunket Society, lived in the house from 1921 to 1924. Katherine was 15 years old when the above photograph was taken.

Alexander Turnbull Library, Hardwick collection, F8611¼

KATHERINE MANSFIELD BIRTHPLACE

Graham Stewart

The South Island

Total area: 150437 km^2
Maori name: Te Waka o Maui (Maui's canoe);
Te Wahipounamu (the place of greenstone)

Alexander Turnbull Library, ½110311F

Gladys M. Goodall, Laurence Eagle collection

Loading timber onto schooners at Havelock in May 1910.

Main Road Havelock (State Highway 6) in the early 1960s.

Havelock is at the head of Pelorus Sound, 36 km west of Picton, where today the waterfront on the Kaituna Estuary is covered with rows of marina berths. It was once a thriving gold-mining town (Wakamarina goldfields 1864) and then a timber town. It prides itself as the 'greenshell mussel capital of the world'. Mussels are farmed nearby, and scallops are dredged from the seabed. Two famous New Zealand-born scientists, Ernest Rutherford and William Pickering, attended the Havelock Primary School. This small hamlet is the gateway to Pelorus and Kenepuru Sounds.

Abel Tasman sailed past d'Urville Island in 1642, followed by French and Russian explorers. In January 1770 James Cook arrived in Ship Cove where he first claimed British Sovereignty. On four other occasions Cook used Ship Cove as his base.

Graham Stewart

The Marlborough and Nelson region

Picton provides the sea link between the North and South Islands at the head of Queen Charlotte Sound. The port town of the Marlborough Sounds, it was first settled by the Te Ati Awa tribe with the Europeans arriving in 1840.

Above and below: The Picton waterfront showing Oxleys Hotel a century apart on the corner of London Quay and Wellington Street. The façade of the old hotel has been incorporated into the new multi-storey development.

Graham Stewart

Above: the *Arahura* prepares to sail.

Right: The *Kaitaki* berths at Picton while in the foreground the Strait Shipping Company's *Monte Stello* unloads heavy transporters. Strait Shipping operates a competitive road and passenger service between Picton and Wellington with their two ships, *Monte Stello* and the *Santa Regina*.

Graham Stewart

Graham Stewart collection

The first purpose-built ferry for the Wellington-to-Picton service was the Union Steam Ship Company twin-funnel *Tamahine* (*above*), known affectionately as 'Tam'. The *Tamahine* always had a slight list to port and was known to corkscrew in heavy seas, making many passengers seasick on the four-hour, 92 km journey across Cook Strait. This ship served for 37 years from 1925 to August 1962, making on average six crossings each week. The *Tamahine* could carry 637 passengers. In 1962 the government placed in service the first road-rail ferry, the *Aramoana* (above right), which gave trucking companies the freedom to drive trucks the full length of the country and linked the railway system between the islands.

Since the *Aramoana* (1962-1983) was commissioned, many road-rail ferries have followed: *Aranui* (1966-1984), *Arahanga* (1972-2000), *Aratika* (1974-1999), *Arahura* (1983 -   ), *Aratere* (1998-   ), *Kaitaki,* roll-on/roll-off ferry, no rail deck (2005 -   ). There have also been four catamaran roll-on, roll-off fast ferries, a service that finished in April 2005. The *Condor 10, Condor Vitesse,* the *Lynx* (*Incat 057*) and *Incat 046.*

Graham Stewart

Alexander Turnbull Library, ½031025F

The *Edwin Fox*, built in Calcutta of teak in 1853, is preserved in a purpose-built dry dock at Dunbar Wharf. It is the ninth oldest ship in the world and the last surviving ship to carry convicts to Australia. The photograph shows the *Edwin Fox* alongside an unidentified ship at Picton in 1897.

Graham Stewart

Blenheim is the main centre of the Marlborough region, 28 km south of Picton. Once a leading pastoral region, Marlborough has become New Zealand's largest wine-producing province, across the gravel Wairau plains which were first used in pre-European times by Maori to grow kumara. Blenheim was founded in 1856 and became the provincial capital of Marlborough in 1865.

Facing page: The Cleghorn Memorial Band Rotunda of 1903 survives in the town centre in Market Place.

Left: The clock from the tower of the old Government Buildings has been incorporated into an ornate tower within the same complex in the centre of town.

Alexander Turnbull Library, Eph E aviation 1930s-01

Alexander Turnbull Library, ½046239G

Blenheim, first known as 'The Beaver', was named by Governor Sir Thomas Gore Browne to commemorate the victory of the Duke of Marlborough over the French in 1704.

Above right: Market Street has slowly been transformed since the 1920s with the demolition of the old colonial wooden buildings, replaced with modern retail buildings, cobbled street surfaces, one-way traffic flows and the return of bicycle stands in the streets.

Graham Stewart

James Taylor collection

Government Buildings & Cleghorn Memorial, Blenheim

Dr George Cleghorn was a Blenheim surgeon at Wairau Hospital (1877-1900). Among his many achievements were the first successful appendectomy and neurosurgical operations performed in New Zealand. He imported the first x-ray machine into New Zealand for use at Wairau Hospital.

Graham Stewart

Nelson Provincial Museum, c2631

Alexander Turnbull Library, F3391 ½

Nelson, at the head of Tasman Bay, was one of Edward Gibbon Wakefield's New Zealand Company settlements when founded. The Maori name Wakatu was soon changed to the hero of Trafalgar, Nelson. By mid-1842 the population had grown to 2000 settlers and in 1858 became New Zealand's first city when Queen Victoria decreed that 'the said Town of Nelson shall be a City'. German settlers had arrived in the mid-1840s to work land at Upper Moutere, establishing vineyards and orchards. The fertile lands surrounding Nelson have continued to produce horticulture, the first apples being exported to the United Kingdom in 1911. The district is bountiful with raspberries, boysenberries, strawberries, kiwifruit and apples.

Above: Two horse-drawn city buses (trams) in Hardy Street at the intersection with Trafalgar Street after Moses Crewdson had purchased the Nelson to Port horse tramway line in 1872.

Above: No. 2 city bus (tram) heading along Hardy Street in 1885. The Hardy and Rutherford Street intersection is in the foreground.

Graham Stewart

Graham Stewart collection

Trafalgar Street, Nelson, N.Z. showing Cathedral & Council Chambers.   Photo by F.N. Jones Jur

Construction of the art deco Christ Church Anglican Cathedral began in 1925 and was not completed until 1965. The building was consecrated in 1972, 47 years after the laying of the foundation stone. It is the third church on the site since 1842.

Graham Stewart

Nelson Provincial Museum, C1735

A horse-drawn tram waiting outside the Ship Hotel on Wakefield Quay in the mid-1870s. Nelson takes the honour of operating the first street horse-drawn tramway service in New Zealand, from the corner of Hardy and Trafalgar Streets to the port from 7 May 1862 to 1901. These were the years when one horsepower was represented by one horse and everything moved at a slow tempo, the horses plodding along at a walking pace. Wakefield Quay, with modern apartment blocks, now moves at a fast pace.

Graham Stewart

Motueka on the Nelson-to-Collingwood road (State Highway 60) is 47 km north-west of Nelson in the centre of the Tasman fruit-growing district. Motueka was the second town in the area to be settled, in 1842, and was created a borough in 1900. The name of the town was Motu weka (motu: a small wood or bush island; weka: woodhen).

Over the winding Takaka hill or Marble Mountain, is the township of Takaka, 103 km north-west of Nelson in the heart of Golden Bay. Golden Bay, between Separation Point and Farewell Spit, was discovered by Abel Tasman in 1642 and named Murderers' Bay after four of his crew were killed in battle with Maori. D'Urville in 1827 called it Massacre Bay, and when coal was found at Takaka in 1842 it was briefly called Coal Bay. Finally, when gold was discovered at Collingwood in 1857 the name Golden Bay was adopted.

Above and below: High Street, Motueka, a century apart. The road is now part of State Highway 60.

Above: The Junction Hotel, Takaka, on a busy day in February 1922. The photograph is dated 2/2/22.
Below: The second Junction Hotel on this site was opened in 1954.

This most unusual limestone formation south-west of Collingwood off the Bainham Road, a few kilometres from Rockville, is known as 'the Devil's Boots'. On each side of the road these two pedestals of limestone support long overhangs. It looks as if two gigantic upturned boots are sticking up out of the ground, looking quite bizarre.

Above: A lovely 1880s period piece of a photographer with a camera on a tripod taking a photograph of a horse and cart, watched by a man on his horse, while two women sit on the grass in the foreground reading.

Looking down on Tasman Street between 1886 and 1891.

Alexander Turnbull Library, ½032612F

Collingwood, at the mouth of the Aorere River, was named after Nelson's second-in-command, Admiral Lord Collingwood. The first gold discovery in the South Island was made in the Aorere River in 1857. In the early boom years it was a busy port with supplies arriving and timber, coal, flax, butter and cheese being shipped out. In January 1858 the town was declared a Port of Entry with a harbour-master and a customs officer. The first wharf at Williams Street was built in 1859; exports continued into the 1960s, the Collingwood Harbour Board being disbanded in the late 1950s.

Fires have haunted the village. The first destroyed the ramshackle gold town in 1859 when it was named Gibbstown, after an early resident. In 1897 the Institute and Library burnt; the great fire of 1904 reduced every building on Tasman Street to rubble; in 1923 a grocery and two drapery stores perished; 1930 saw eight buildings at the north end of town destroyed, including the Collingwood Hotel; in 1938 the public hall and a store went up in flames, and in 1967 the Post Office Hotel, the Memorial Hall (picture theatre and library) and a store were all engulfed by fire.

Collingwood is the gateway to the Heaphy Track in the Kahurangi National Park, an old Maori route. It is a walk of 82 km to Karamea on the West Coast.

All communities around New Zealand have memorials to those who gave their lives in conflict. The Collingwood War Memorial was dedicated on 25 April 1923.
Left: The Cenotaph, 25 April 2008.

Graham Stewart

Graham Stewart

Baron Rutherford of Nelson (1871-1937), Sir Ernest Rutherford, was the first person to split the atom, giving the world a new source of energy. This monument at Spring Grove near Brightwater marks the birthplace of the father of nuclear physics and a Nobel laureate. He was educated at Foxhill (1876-1881) and Havelock (1882-1886) primary schools, Nelson College (1887-1889), Canterbury (University) College, Christchurch (1890-1895) and the Cavendish Laboratory, University of Cambridge, England (1895-1898).

M. Earle collection, courtesy Barry O'Donnell

Wakefield was named after Nelson's founder Arthur Wakefield. The post office building (1909) on Edward Street with the cupola makes the building look the most important in town. In the years of the Nelson-to-Glenhope railway (1876-1954), there was a railway level-crossing where State Highway Six passes Edward Street today.

Above: c1910 the local grocer drives his two-horse team with his delivery wagon across the railway level-crossing loaded with produce for his country clients.

Tasman Bay Heritage Trust, Nelson Provincial Museum, c2497

Once a busy railway terminus by the Nelson-West Coast road, State Highway Six, Glenhope, 96 km from Nelson, became the terminus for the railway from Nelson when the line was extended 12 miles from Kiwi on 2 September 1912. The railway station, yards and settlement were built after the land had been cleared of forest and bush. Felled tree stumps in the foreground (above) had been pushed back for the construction of the railway. After travelling from Nelson to Glenhope by train in May 1920, the Prince of Wales dined at Alf Inwood's dining-rooms at Glenhope on his way south. Seven years later, his brother, the Duke of York (later King George VI), also travelled by train from Nelson to Glenhope on his way to the West Coast. Amid political protests, the line closed in June 1954. Today, only one railway house and the skeleton of the old station building remain.

Graham Stewart

Murchison, on State Highway Six, is the southern gateway to the Nelson region, 125 km south of Nelson, 95 km east of Westport. It was surveyed in 1865 as a supply centre for the gold-rush town of Lyell in the Buller Gorge. It was named by Scottish geologist Julius von Haast after the nearby Mount Murchison. With a population of about 300 at the time, the district was rocked on the morning of 17 June 1929 by New Zealand's worst earthquake since European settlement, at a strength of 7.8 on the Richter scale. The land mass was completely altered with hillsides falling into valleys and several homes and their occupants buried; roads, bridges and buildings collapsed. The town was left virtually uninhabitable with 17 lives lost. The epicenter was in the Lyell Range a few kilometres west of Murchison. The earthquake was felt through both islands.

Above: Locals feed dogs left homeless after the 1929 earthquake, in Fairfax Street. The two-storey wooden hotel on the corner of Waller Street still trades as the Hampden Hotel.

Westland
The West Coast

Alexander Turnbull Library, ½006437G

Graham Stewart

Above: Guests pose for a photograph c1910, before boarding their charabanc outside the Karamea Hotel. Built in 1876 and completely rebuilt in 1906, two generations of the original owner, James Simpson, ran the hotel for over 100 years.

Karamea is at the end of the road, 100 km north of Westport, at the northern end of the South Island's West Coast. Just up the road is the southern entrance to the Heaphy Track through the Kahurangi National Park to Nelson Province. A remote part of the West Coast, there is evidence of Maori occupation, and the first European and Chinese were there in the 1860s in search of gold. The lifting of the seabed by the 1929 earthquake made the port inoperable.

Below: As far as the road goes north on the West Coast is the entrance to the Heaphy Track.

Graham Stewart

cline — Denniston   D. Maloney, Photo.

Graham Stewart

Brian McClintock collection

A restored coal wagon and recreated track work at the top of the incline, 2008.

Denniston is 24 km north of Westport and is now a coal-mining ghost town with an unbelievable history. In the 1870s the problem of transporting coal from this hilltop mine was solved by the building of a counter-balanced cableway railway; the descending wagon full of coal pulled an empty wagon up the incline. The combined vertical descent of the two inclines was 518 metres spread over 1.67 km, making the overall gradient from top to bottom 1 in 3.22. The loaded wagons could reach speeds of up to 50 km/h on the down grades. An average of 15 wagons an hour descended the incline. The last spike ceremony at the top took place on 24 October 1879 when the mountain railway was described as an engineering wonder of New Zealand. The mine on the Mount Rochfort plateau was 600 metres above sea level, and this was where the families of the miners lived, on the barren hilltop exposed to the bitter winters, a self-contained village with its own community buildings and a school. The first coal wagon made the descent in April 1880. Over the decades the incline handled an average 120 tons of coal an hour until closed on 16 August 1967.

Alexander Turnbull Library, John Pascoe, F13332¼

An empty wagon climbs the extreme gradient of the incline as Denniston school pupils and their teacher, who lived on 'the hill' in 1944, smile for the photographer.

Mark Cole

Left: This photograph of the closing days of the incline in June 1967 shows a wagon beyond the brake house being made ready for the journey down the incline.

In 2007 the Department of Conservation started to recreate the Brakehead site at the top of the incline with the laying of the former railway track network and placing on the tracks three restored coal hopper wagons as part of an industrial heritage display for tourists.

Historical novels by Jenny Pattrick, *The Denniston Rose* (2003) and *Heart of Coal* (2004), give readers an insight into the harsh living conditions of mining families who lived on the hill at Denniston.

Below: The reincarnation of the old Brakehead bins area in 2008.

Graham Stewart

Graham Stewart

Westport was once a bustling gold and coal town with its river port built on the eastern bank at the mouth of the Buller River for the export of these precious nuggets from the land. In June 1861, 16 miners arrived on the *Jane* and settled on the present site of Westport. On 29 January the following year, the *Tasmanian Maid* became the first vessel to cross the bar. Most of the population of 200 in 1862 was Maori. The name is said to date from 1862 after Westport, on Clew Bay, in Connaught, Ireland. Today it is Buller's main commercial centre and has retained many of its Victorian buildings.

Palmerston Street. Westport. F.G.R.6509.

James Taylor collection

Above: Palmerston Street c1919 shows the old post office and tower built in 1912. The tower was a memorial to the Rt Hon. Richard John Seddon (Premier 1893-1906) which collapsed on 17 June 1929, a victim of the Murchison earthquake.

Facing page: The building with the curved Edwardian shop verandah on the left and in the above photograph, still stands, although now nicely decorated with colourful hanging baskets of flowers.

Right: The Municipal Council Chambers inherited the old post office town clock.

Graham Stewart

HAWK'S CRAG, Buller Gorge. *New Zealand Tourist Bureau (Copyright),*
Series 51—West Coast, N.Z. Kerry and Co., Publishers, Sydney.

Graham Stewart collection

Hawk's Crag, Buller Gorge, N. Z.

Hawks Craig Buller Gorge. F.G.R. 6544.

Simon Crawford collection

Graham Stewart

Hawks Crag has been a popular subject for postcards since the only form of motive power
was the four-legged horse and when postcards had to be hand-coloured.

Hawks Crag is 33 km from Westport on State Highway Six. The road follows the course of the Buller River, which has the greatest flood discharge in New Zealand, from its headwaters on Lake Rotoiti. The road passes through steep-sided gorges where in some places it is reduced to one-way traffic. A natural canopy over the road, carved out of conglomerate rock, is a feature of this area. The Maori name for the river is Kawatiri, believed to mean 'deep and swift', an apt description of this mighty river.

Graham Stewart

Alexander Turnbull Library. ½025252F

Graham Stewart

A lamp standard on Broadway, modelled on the original standard, commemorates the fact that Reefton homes had electricity before many of the fashionable suburbs in London and New York. Power was supplied from sunset to sunrise and each Tuesday when the ladies did the ironing.

Dawson's Hotel on Broadway c1880s (left). Established 1874, it was one of 17 pubs that once quenched the town's thirst and was the first hotel in the southern hemisphere to be lit by electric light.

Reefton is the only inland town of any size on the Coast, a pioneer settlement in the Inangahua River Valley founded on gold and coal in the 1870s. It is 78 km north-east of Greymouth. In August 1888 it was the first settlement in the southern hemisphere to install a public hydro-electric station, using water from the Inangahua River to light the town and the streets. Many of the town's restored buildings date from the gold-rush days. It is situated in the heart of the Victoria Conservation Park, New Zealand's largest at 180,000 hectares. The road over the Lewis Pass opened on 30 October 1937.

Graham Stewart

Courtesy Jane Wells of 'Formerly' the Blackball Hilton Hotel

Blackball miners outside the Miners' Hall (centre) in Hart Street during a fall of snow in 1931. The original Blackball Hotel (above left) was demolished in the 1950s, and in the distance is the hotel known today as 'Formerly' the Blackball Hilton.

Blackball, named after the Blackball Shipping Line of England, is 22 km north-east of Greymouth on the Grey River. It started life as a small gold town in 1864, and in 1893 the first coal mine opened. It was once a bustling and notorious village. A strike by coalminers in 1908 won them a half-hour lunch break and led to the formation of the New Zealand Labour Party.

The Blackball Hotel, which opened as the Dominion Hotel in July 1910, made world headlines when the owners renamed it 'The Blackball Hilton' in 2000. Following much publicity and threats of legal action by the Hilton worldwide hotel chain, the owners added the word 'Formerly' to the name on the outside of the hotel. Miners' draught and dark ale are on tap, advertised as the genuine West Coast beer.

Graham Stewart

Graham Stewart

Alexander Turnbull Library, ½011550F

Graham Stewart collection

In 1866 the discovery of gold in Charleston, 26 km south-west of Westport, brought shiploads of prospectors from all around Australasia. Within a few months a town was born with everything from banks to butcher shops to cater for the population that reached 12,000. At the height of the boom there were 93 hotels in Charleston.

The last of the original hotels was the European, built by Charles Weitzel in 1866, one of only three that were two-storey. The European even had a dance floor with the name of the pub reflecting its clientele. The hotels were known to stay open 24 hours at times and to offer dance hall entertainment in the evening, to cater for men who worked long and hard hours on the diggings.

Right: The European Hotel, third down the street from the corner, when Arthur King was the publican. The store with the verandah on the left of the European was where Robert Hannah started his shoe business.

Below: The old European Hotel was just standing and no more in the 1970s. On the other side of the road is the tavern (in the distance) that took the historic name and is still trading. Like an old soldier, the old pub never died, it just faded away.

New Zealand Herald

Punakaiki pancake rocks and blowholes at Dolomite Point in the heart of the Paparoa National Park. These unusual formations are the result of heaving swells from the Tasman Sea over thousands of years on the stratified limestone rocks. The power of the sea, as it surges into the sea caves, regularly sends blasts of sea spray through blowholes skyward

Left: A classic posed photograph taken by a photographer of note, John Pascoe. A home guardsman during the Second World War stands guard, waiting for the enemy to appear over the horizon.

Simon Crawford collection

Graham Stewart

Greymouth's position at the mouth of the Grey River is the obvious source of its name. Before its founding, a Maori pa, Mawhera, stood by the mouth of the river. Settled by Europeans as a gold-diggers' camp in the 1860s, it became a coal and timber exporting port and the largest town on the Coast. The river was named by Thomas Brunner after Sir George Grey (Premier 1845-1853, 1861-1868).

Above: Like many town clocks around New Zealand, the clock on the tower of the old post office was placed in storage when the tower was demolished in 1945 as an earthquake risk.

Above right: The old clock of 1908 vintage now looks out over the town again from a tower completed in November 1992 at the corner of Mawhera Quay and Tainui Street on the city's flood bank, named 'The Great Wall of Greymouth'.

Right: Looking down Tainui Street from where the town clock stands today. Compare the upper photograph, c1900s, with Hansom cabs outside the Victoria Tearooms waiting for fares, while in the distance the old post office tower has a flag flying from the masthead.

Merle Sneddon collection

Graham Stewart

Alexander Turnbull Library, James Ring, G27049½

Cyclists pedal down Tainui Street past Mackay Street in a grand convoy on what must have been a special occasion, judging by people standing on the sidewalks and the crowd on the verandah of Revingtons Hotel down the street opposite Guinness Street, c1895. Everyone was wearing a hat, the ladies were in their long skirts and the men were all wearing ties.

Graham Stewart

Five Union Steam Ship Company colliers load coal in the heyday of the shipment of coal from Greymouth.

Gavin McLean collection

Robin Smith, Laurence Eagle collection

Graham Stewart

Left: The upper-truss, wooden-structured 19th century road-bridge on iron cylindrical piles was replaced with the new Cobden road bridge which opened on 9 August 1975.
The last train crossed the old, upper-truss railway bridge on 28 May 2006 – the first train across the new bridge was on 2 June 2006.

Graham Stewart

History House, Greymouth

Greymouth was an isolated railway town handling mainly coal from the mines to the port until the Otira tunnel opened in August 1923, linking the West Coast railway network to the rest of the South Island railway system. The railway tracks that once ran alongside the wharves on the Grey River were removed in 1989 for the building of the flood bank.

Above: The first through express from Greymouth to Christchurch departs on 7 August 1923. The old semaphore signal gantry has gone, as has the network of tracks along the wharves, but the signal box remains.

Below: The TranzAlpine departs Greymouth on its 231 km journey to Christchurch. This coast-to-coast tourist train is claimed to be one of the world's great rail journeys.

Graham Stewart

eremakau, N. Z.

I.A.T. Terry collection

Graham Stewart

Hocken Collections, Uare Taoka o Hakena, University of Otago, E5522/22A

Passage across rivers for early settlers often meant a feat to get to the other side with dry feet. The problem of crossing the Taramakau River, once rich with greenstone and gold, was solved with the building of a wire tram, as it was known. It was built in 1877 and was still in operation in the early 1900s. People travelling south from Greymouth and north from Hokitika and Kumara by horse tram were carried across the river by this suspended cableway cage.

Right: The Tramway Hotel and Store by the wire tram terminus was handy for a drink while waiting for the wire tram.

Below: The impressive combined rail-road bridge was built in the early 1890s, and the rail line between Greymouth and Hokitika opened on 18 December 1893.

Graham Stewart collection

Graham Stewart

Otira was a bustling railway town after the line opened from Jackson in November 1900. Passengers transferred at Otira to stagecoaches for a bone-shaking and nerve-racking trip up and over the Southern Alps to the Canterbury Plains. It was to be another 23 years before the Alps were conquered with the 8554-metre Otira railway tunnel to Arthur's Pass. Because the gradient through the tunnel was 1 in 33, electric traction was installed, as the bulk of the heavy rail traffic was from the West Coast. Electric traction was replaced in 1998 with diesel-electric after new ventilation systems were placed in the tunnel, so that coal trains from the Coast could be used up the steep grade.

Above left: Horse-drawn coaches prepare to leave the Terminus Hotel in April 1911 for the gruelling journey along the narrow, winding road over the Southern Alps, often having to battle snowdrifts or ford streams in flood.

Left: The village is now privately owned; the hotel is now named the Otira Hotel and is still the meeting place for locals. A coal train rumbles past in the background.

Otira has two meanings, either 'out of the sun' or 'food for a journey', and both are apt, especially the latter when it was a busy railway stopping place with refreshment rooms.

The Otira viaduct on State Highway 73 took just on three years to build and was opened by Prime Minister Jenny Shipley on 6 November 1999. It was designed by Beca Carter Hollings and Ferner and built by Transit New Zealand at a cost of $25 million. The construction contractor was McConnell Smith Limited. A three-kilometre section of the top portion of the old road known as the ZigZag has been retired, its seal and culverts removed to enable natural vegetation to return.

Graham Stewart

Simon Crawford collection

Running from the Waimakariri in the east to the Taramakau River in the west was one of the passes used by Maori for greenstone (pounamu) trade. The gorge, then known as Otitira, was first used by Europeans as a walking track to the Westland goldfields. When Sir Arthur Dobson discovered a coach route, it took only 18 months, including the fierce winter months, for men to carve a coach road from Christchurch to the West Coast. It opened on 20 March 1866.

Hokitika is 43 km south-west of Greymouth and was the fifth largest town in the land in gold days. It was the busiest port in New Zealand in 1865-1867, apart from Auckland, when the town mushroomed with masses of settlers arriving to seek their fortune. 102 hotels, casinos, theatres and even an opera house seating 1400 were to be found in downtown Hokitika.

Left: The clock tower, the landmark of Hokitika, was unveiled on 3 June 1903 by Mrs Seddon, wife of Premier Richard John Seddon, and commemorates the fallen of the Boer War and the coronation of Edward VII.

Graham Stewart

Graham Stewart

James Taylor collection

Above: The Carnegie Free Public Library building, opened in June 1908 with a gold key, was one of 18 libraries built in New Zealand through the generosity of Scottish-American philanthropist Andrew Carnegie. The library served the town until closed in April 1975. Interest in this grand building, designed by Nelson architect A.R. Griffin, saw it restored and re-opened in May 1998. It is now the home of the Westland Visitor Information Office and the West Coast Historical Museum.

Richard John Seddon (1845-1906) is New Zealand's longest serving premier, holding office for 13 years and one month. He was born in Lancashire, went to Australia where he worked unsuccessfully in the Victorian gold fields, then to the West Coast diggings where he failed again as a prospector. He then opened a store which was successful enough to obtain a liquor licence he transferred to Kumara. He was the first mayor of Kumara in 1877. In 1879 he became the Member for Hokitika, then a minister of the crown under John Ballance. When Ballance died, he became premier on 1 May 1893, a position he held until his death on 10 June 1906. He was a loyal imperialist, had been a prize-fighter as a young man and was always ready to fight for his causes. His administration made many reforms, including the age pension and free secondary education. He is still remembered by his nickname of 'King Dick'.

Graham Stewart

Alexander Turnbull Library, ½017897

Ross was where New Zealand's largest gold nugget was found in 1909, the 'Honourable Roddy'. It was named after Roderick McKenzie, the Minister of Mines and weighed 3.09 kilograms. The nugget was purchased by the Government and given as a coronation gift to King George V in May 1910. Gold was found here in all forms: alluvial deposits, quartz and beach sand gold. All types of mining techniques were used at Ross: sluice box, cradle, ground sluicing, hydraulic, dredges, horse whim and Chinese mining.

Above: Aylmer Street adjacent to the gold mines c1860s, when everyone in town must have been at church as only one person is visible on the street.

Below: The junction of Aylmer Street with Moorhouse Street and Grimmond Avenue today.

Below: Aylmer Street with the Empire Hotel (right). The original Empire of 1866 was felled by fire and rebuilt in 1908. It has survived from the gold days when 21 hotels traded in the town.

Graham Stewart

Graham Stewart

The Franz Josef and Fox Glaciers – from the top of the Southern Alps these great cascades of ice valleys move slowly down the mountains into the bush-clad rain forest valleys below to only 250 metres above sea level. Both glaciers are within the Westland Tai Poutini National Park. Glaciers descend at the rate of one to four metres a day. Nowhere in the world are there such accessible glaciers.

Above: The mighty Franz Josef viewed from the base of the walking track.

The Franz Josef was named after the Austro-Hungarian emperor by Julius von Haast, the first European to explore the glacier in 1865. It had been reported by Leonard Harper in 1857 and was first known as Victoria.

Right: Edwardian tourists enjoy a walk on the Franz Josef Glacier in 1906.

FRANCIS JOSEPH GLACIER

Alexander Turnbull Library, James Ring, PAI-o-436162

Alexander Turnbull Library, Eph-A-tourism-Franz 1935-01

TRAVEL IN NEW ZEALAND
at the FRANZ JOSEF *Glacier*

A GLEAMING JEWEL *in the* MOUNTAIN SIDE

Graham Stewart collection

Above: The Fox Glacier Hotel opened in 1929, was restored in 2007 and is in the heart of the Fox township. It is known by locals as The Fox.

Below: The Fox Glacier Hotel today houses the Mountain Goats Bakery and Café and the Climbers' Rest Bar with its big fireplace, a haunt for locals and tourists.

Alexander Turnbull Library, 1/1 017564F

Above: The old Tourist Corporation Hotel at Franz Josef, where everyone stayed in the days before motels, was burnt to the ground on 15 August 1954.

Below: State Highway Six at the Franz Josef village is stacked with visitors and cars the year round.

Graham Stewart

Graham Stewart

The Fox Glacier, 25 km south of Franz Josef, was named after Sir William Fox who visited the area while premier. The glacier is 13 km long and reaches a height of 2800 metres.

Robin Smith, William Main collection

Haast is 117 km south-west of the Fox Glacier, passing Bruce Bay, Lake Paringa and Lake Moeraki on the way. It was named after the explorer and geologist Julius von Haast who was there in 1863. The Haast Pass Road, Tioripatea, meaning 'clear path' in Maori, was a Maori war trail and also a walking track used by Maori to carry greenstone to Otago. This road, which links the West Coast to Otago, took 30 years to build and was not opened until 8 November 1960. It passes through the Mount Aspiring National Park and is the southern gateway to the West Coast. Travelling from the West Coast mountainous wild terrain to the placid grasslands of Central Otago or vice versa presents an amazing contrast of nature.

It is a paradise for bird-watchers with fantail, tui, bellbird, pigeon, silvereye, grey warbler, parakeet, falcon, kaka, kiwi and morepork all in abundance in the lowland forests. The drive over the Haast Pass runs through rainforests, wetlands, lakes, glacier-fed rivers and white-water rapids. The area has been declared equal to the Grand Canyon, the Great Barrier Reef and Mount Everest as a natural treasure of world standing.

Above: The Gates of the Haast Bridge in the upper Haast Gorge is a one-way bridge and one of New Zealand's longest at 737 metres. It is the third bridge across the Haast River from the Coast.

North Canterbury

Hanmer Springs, an alpine spa village in the South Island high country in North Canterbury, is 370 metres above sea level, 130 km north of Christchurch, and is the South Island's main thermal resort. The therapeutic thermal waters, known to Maori as 'Waitapu' (sacred waters), were located in 1859 by William Jones, a farm manager from the Culverden area. First a sanatorium, it evolved into a health resort where people have flocked for the benefits of the natural mineral waters and the alpine air for decades. The temperature of the mineral waters ranges from 33 to 42 Celsius.

Above: From the bathhouses c1915 to the new entrance buildings of today and the pools of the 1950s (*below*), it has been a long journey of progress from the first dressing shed in 1871 and the first bathhouse built in 1883.

Merle Sneddon collection

Kaikoura in Maori rightly means 'to eat crayfish', kai 'food' and koura 'crayfish', where Maori first found and feasted on crayfish before the whalers arrived and set up camp. The years have passed, and in 1987 whale-watching started as a tourist enterprise, now attracting people from around the world to view at close range these mighty mammals of the ocean. The township, 183 km north of Christchurch, is on the edge of the Pacific Ocean, nestled between the ocean and the steeply rising Seaward Kaikoura Range.

Above and below: The old Adelphi Hotel on West End is now the Adelphi Lodge and Backpackers.

Captain Charles Upham (1908-1994) Victoria Cross & Bar. The Victoria Cross was awarded for sustained gallantry, skill and leadership on Crete between 22 and 30 May 1941. The Bar to the Victoria Cross was awarded for outstanding gallantry and magnificent leadership as a company commander on attack on Ruweisat Ridge on 14-15 July 1942. After the war Upham farmed in the Hurunui district.

Graham Stewart

Graham Stewart

New Zealand Memories, courtesy Kaikoura Historical Society

Above: On the edge of the coast where the Pacific Ocean pounds the foreshore south of Kaikoura on State Highway One are two twin tunnels, the first being the Parititahi tunnels. The first Parititahi tunnel was cut through by miners employed by the Public Works Department and opened for traffic in late 1901.

Right: Alan Turner drives a two-horse team from the Club Hotel through the first Parititahi in 1910.

Below: The second set of tunnels, when driving south, is the Raramai tunnels. The first was tunnelled through 56 yards of hard rock in seven months in the late 1890s.

Graham Stewart

Graham Stewart collection

Merle Sneddon collection

Rangiora is the principal town of North Canterbury, a farming service centre which started as a sawmilling town in 1852. It is 27 km north of Christchurch, 11 km north-west of Kaiapoi, between the Waimakariri and Ashley Rivers, inland from State Highway One.

Above: Looking east along High Street showing the second post office and tower, opened in December 1887. The building was criticised as unsightly, more fitting as a fortress on the road to Kabul. The clock was installed in 1892 after a fund-raising appeal by the mayor. The third post office, which still stands today, was opened in September 1936.

Kaiapoi is on the banks of the Kaiapoi River, a tributary of the Waimakariri River. Once a river port, it is 20 km north of Christchurch. The town's department store, Blackwell, was established in 1871 by George Blackwell who emigrated from England in 1840. The store has been run by five generations of Blackwells, and a till purchased in 1885 is still in use.

Above: The main street looking south from the old iron bridge (1885-1946) which replaced the original wooden swing bridge. Brown's Temperance Hotel is on the right.

Graham Stewart

Christchurch

William and John Deans were the first to farm the Canterbury Plains successfully in 1843; they named the Avon River after the Scottish river in Ayrshire. In 1848 the Government purchased more than eight million acres of land from Maori which led to the formation of the Canterbury Association, an Anglican enterprise in partnership with Edward Gibbon Wakefield's New Zealand Company. The Canterbury Pilgrims arrived on the first four ships in December 1850 – the *Charlotte Jane, Cressy, Randolph* and *Sir George Seymour*. The majority had travelled steerage and on arrival at Lyttelton, had to face the arduous walk up the roughly formed bridle path over the Port Hills and down to the site for their promised land. The Canterbury Association was led by John Robert Godley and the city's name is derived from Godley's college at Oxford. The four avenues that were the original boundaries of the city area were named after the founding fathers: Bealey, Moorhouse, Fitzgerald and Rolleston.

John M. Bettle collection

Christchurch citizens gathered in Cathedral Square in December 1900 for the 50th anniversary procession of the Canterbury Province. The double-decker tramway trailer No. 10, in the centre of the photograph, was the first tramway vehicle to be built in New Zealand.

A public telephone box in Cathedral Square in August 1912. The notice on the door states '2P in the Slot': it cost two pennies to make a call at the time. Similar telephone boxes have again been placed on the pavements of Worcester Boulevard.

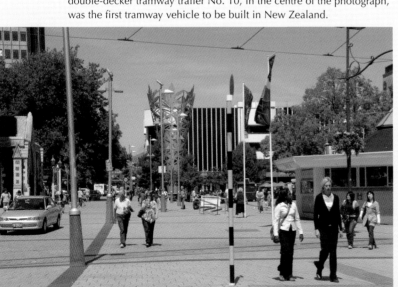

Graham Stewart collection

A 'Yank' type tram arrives in The Square, a cabbie with his Brougham waits for a fare while his horse enjoys a rest, and a young mother pushes her cane high-wheel pram past the Cathedral in the 1920s. The Square is now a pedestrian area and used by open-air entertainers and as a craft market on a number of days each week.

Graham Stewart

Alexander Turnbull Library, PA1 F0202O.4

A horse-tram driver walks his four-horse team to waiting double-decker trams of the New Brighton Tramway Company (1887-1905) c1890s. The driver will lift the heavy swingle-tree attached to the front of the leading tram and couple it to the trace chains and leather straps linked to the horse collars. The upper deck was a popular place to sit for an elevated view of the passing scene. The first trams started running from The Square to the railway station on 9 March 1880; the first electrics arrived on 6 June 1905.

Christchurch Cathedral was a long-term building project: the foundation stone was laid in 1864, it was consecrated and opened in 1881, and another 23 years passed before it was completed in 1904. It is the landmark of Christchurch, a fine example of Gothic revival architecture designed by Sir George Gilbert Scott who designed London's Albert Memorial. Local architect Benjamin Woolfield Mountfort added many features, including balconies to the tower and the western porch.

Graham Stewart

Those who witnessed the last electric trams leave Cathedral Square on Saturday, 11 September 1954 would find it unbelievable that 41 years later on Saturday, 4 February 1995, electric trams would be running through Cathedral Square again. The Christchurch tourist tramway uses a mix of restored Christchurch trams and former Melbourne trams, together with a restaurant tram which has become a must ride- and-dine for tourists.

Above: To the left is the Venetian Gothic-style post office which opened in July 1879, now overshadowed by the Telecom building. In the centre is the baroque-style Royal Exchange building, opened in May 1905. The architects were Alfred and Sidney Luttrell. The building was redeveloped in the 1930s as the Regent movie theatre, now also dwarfed by new high-rise office buildings. The steel hoops on the upper deck of the tram were a safety precaution to guard against the trolley-pole swinging wildly and striking passengers if it came off the overhead wire.

Kate Sheppard (1848-1934): suffragist, born in Liverpool, educated in Scotland, came to New Zealand in 1869, married a Christchurch storekeeper, led the campaign 'votes for women' and petitions to Parliament, won the right for women to vote in 1893. It was not until 1919 that the law was changed to allow women to stand for Parliament.

Alexander Turnbull Library, Radcliffe collection 6524½

Looking south from the Square at the busy 'bottleneck' area of Colombo Street during the First World War. Double-decker tram No. 26 works the Woolston service, while the Boon-type tram No. 43 heads south bound for Coronation Street. The town is bustling with shoppers. On the right is the Italianate United Service Hotel (1906), built in 1885 as Morten's Building, and demolished in 1990. The modern ANZ building now stands here. The building on the corner of Hereford Street still stands with the upper parapets removed.

Graham Stewart

Elizabeth McCombs (1873-1935): feminist, prohibitionist, first woman elected to Parliament, Christchurch City Councillor 1921-1935, North Canterbury Hospital Board 1921, Christchurch Tramway Board 1927. She unsuccessfully contested Kaiapoi for Labour in 1920 and 1931 and won the Lyttelton seat in a by-election in 1933, caused by her husband's death. She died in office, and the seat was won by her son Terence. Other Christchurch women who made history were Mabel Howard, the first woman Cabinet Minister in 1947, and Dame Ngaio Marsh, novelist and playwright.

Green and Hahn, Graham Stewart collection

Hereford and High Streets in the late 1920s, looking east from Colombo Street. The Fisher building (1880) in the centre is a classic example of Venetian Gothic architecture and was designed by W.B. Armson. It was built for the Rev. T.R. Fisher who leased the shops and offices. A policeman directs traffic, mainly bicycles, while a coupé motorcar with a 'dickey' seat waits in the foreground. Horse-drawn vehicles were still being used to deliver goods around the city.

Below: Since this photograph was taken the 'Flour Power' sculpture in the form of a wheat sheaf which symbolises Canterbury agriculture has been placed by the tree on the right.

Graham Stewart

Alexander Turnbull Library, PA coll 717189

It started as a minor fire in the basement of J. Ballantyne and Company's department store on the corner of Colombo and Cashel Streets during a shopping afternoon on 18 November 1947. It soon spread to an inferno with a death toll of 41. It was the most shocking tragedy by fire recorded in New Zealand, before the days of fire drills and fire sprinklers. From lessons learnt, New Zealand has become a much safer place with fire-prevention training and strict regulations.

Graham Stewart

Graham Stewart collection

Graham Stewart

The cast-iron clock tower was imported from England in 1859 for the Provincial Government Buildings but not erected until 1897, when it was placed on a stone base at the junction where High, Lichfield and Manchester Streets meet by the Christchurch City Council to commemorate the Diamond Jubilee of Queen Victoria's reign. It then became known as the Diamond Jubilee Clock Tower.   In 1930, because of traffic congestion, it was moved to the Salisbury, Montreal and Victoria Streets junction at the other end of town.

Graham Stewart

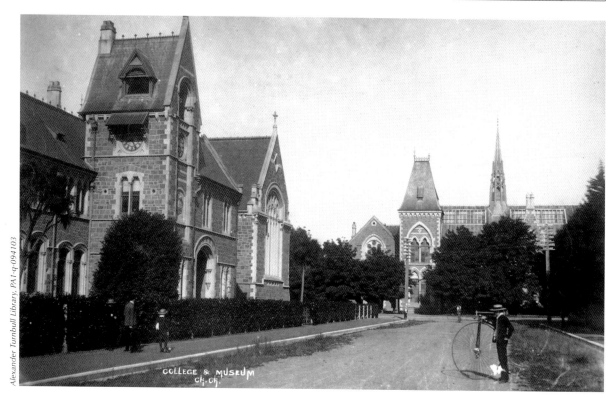

Alexander Turnbull Library, PA1-q-094103

COLLEGE & MUSEUM
CH. CH.

Worcester Street, showing the clock tower building in the foreground of the Canterbury University College. Victorian Collegiate Gothic in design, it was opened on 7 June 1877; the clock was installed in August 1878. Beyond (centre left) is the Great Hall (1882). The materials used for the buildings were basalt stone from the Port Hills and limestone from Oamaru. In the distance (facing) is the Canterbury Museum, opened to the public on 30 September 1870. The former Canterbury University College buildings form what is known today as the Arts Centre. The Canterbury University College was the first to admit women in 1881 and produced the first woman honours graduate in the British Empire. The tourist electric tramway, opened in February 1995, runs down Worcester Boulevard and turns right into Rolleston Avenue.

Graham Stewart

Alexander Turnbull Library, ½049505G

The Victoria Street Bridge across the Avon River, built of stone and cast iron, was opened on 28 September 1864 by the breaking of a bottle of champagne over the bridge. The bridge was widened in 1875 and again in 1885 to its present width. It was closed to road traffic in 1988 for the development of Victoria Square. Tram rails by the restored bridge commemorate 74 years of tram services to Fendalton and the Papanui areas by steam, horse and electric vehicles from 5 June 1880 to 11 September 1954.

Above: A tram for Papanui crosses the bridge c1905. The large fender on the front could scoop cyclist and bike to safety if a cyclist accidentally fell in front of the tram.

Right: On 18 December 1989 the bridge was renamed 'The Hamish Hay Bridge' to honour Sir Hamish Grenfell Hay, mayor of Christchurch from 1974 to 1989. Today the old bridge is enjoyed by pedestrians strolling around Victoria Square.

Graham Stewart

Victoria Street Bridge, Christchurch, N. Z.

P. T. Series. No. 91. A.

Graham Stewart collection

Above: A tram crosses the bridge c1905. The tram is the unique combined passenger and baggage tram, the only one to run in New Zealand. It was built to operate a passenger and baggage service from the Christchurch railway station to Cathedral Square. It later ran a freight service on all lines and in May 1938 was converted to carry staff bicycles between the Falsgrave Street carshed and The Square carshed.

Graham Stewart

Goodman Fielder New Zealand

The Edmonds Baking Powder factory was for many decades in Ferry Road, Woolston, an enterprise started by a young man named Thomas John Edmonds who had arrived on the sailing ship *Waitangi* at Lyttelton in the 1870s. He opened a small grocery store in Christchurch and soon found that his customers were complaining about the unreliable baking powder products of the time.

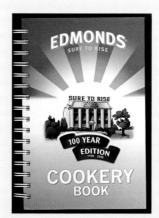

Drawing on the blending experience he had gained while working for a confectioner in London, he began making his own baking powder in the back of his shop. His first batch of 200 tins went on sale in 1879. When questioned by one client as to the superiority of his product, Edmonds is said to have replied, 'It is sure to rise Madam' – and so the famous Edmonds promise was born. In 1908 the first edition of the Edmonds Cookery Book was published. Today it is still New Zealand's most popular cookbook. Thomas Edmonds retired in 1911 but was still around to supervise the building of the factory in 1920 which features on their products. He died in 1932. Amid protests the building was demolished in 1990; the gardens where the building once stood are now maintained by the Christchurch City Council.

Alexander Turnbull Library, Steffano Webb coll. 5463 1/1

Graham Stewart

The Colombo Street bridge over the Avon River was built in 1902 with ornamental street lamps and in 1930 widened to its present width. Trams started running over the bridge, along Bealey Avenue and Barbadoes Street to Edgeware Road in December 1906. The decorative pillars at each end of the bridge have been lowered and art deco-style street lamps and stands installed.

The Oxford Hotel on the left has been on the corner of Colombo Street and Oxford Terrace in various forms since 1862, first as a wooden building. From being the Oxford Family Hotel, it became the Oxford Victualling Company in 1978 and later Oxford on Avon.

Right: In Christchurch the trolley-buses, like the trams, carried prams and pushchairs on the front of the vehicles. Trolley-buses were first introduced in 1931 on the North Beach service and later to Richmond in 1934. All trolley-bus services closed in 1956.

Reginald McGovern

Graham Stewart collection

Looking from Barrington Street to Athelstan Street, Spreydon, in November 1932, a typical 1930s suburban scene shows a combined corner store and dwelling, the boot repairer down Athelstan Street, bicycles, a lone motorcar and a tram arriving at the terminus.

Graham Stewart

Canterbury Museum, 6259

NEW BRIGHTON.

The original Brighton pier (opened 18 January 1894), tearooms building and band rotunda c1915. The tram and trailers have circled the block to load returning beach-goers. The original 210-metre-long wooden pier was demolished in 1965 after being pounded by the Pacific Ocean surf for over 70 years. The new concrete pier (*below*) and complex opened in 1998.

Graham Stewart

W.W. Stewart

Above: In 1950 the province of Canterbury celebrated 100 years. During the centennial celebrations Kitson steam tram No. 7 of 1881 vintage was restored and gave rides hauling two restored old double-decker trailers around Christchurch. During the summer of 1950 the steam tram and trailers ran along the Marine Parade between New Brighton and North Beach.

Below: Looking towards the clock tower from the New Brighton Mall, formerly Seaview Road.

Graham Stewart

Simon Crawford collection

Alexander Turnbull Library, ½006905G

Lyttelton was the home of successive generations of Maori since the 1400s. Cook thought the peninsula was an island and named it after his botanist Sir Joseph Banks. Maori named the harbour Whangaraupo (harbour of the raupo) after the reeds at Governors Bay and Allandale. It became known in the 1830s as Port Cooper and briefly as Port Victoria. When the Canterbury Association decided in 1849 to make it the port for their colonisation of the area, it was named Lyttelton after their chairman, Lord Lyttelton. The name was officially adopted for the harbour in 1857.

It was the gateway to the South Island for travellers by an overnight ferry service that linked Wellington and Lyttelton until September 1976. The bed of the harbour is an extinct volcanic crater; it is now the largest port in the South Island and the seaport for Canterbury. It is connected to Christchurch by New Zealand's oldest rail tunnel, which opened on 9 November 1867, and New Zealand's longest road tunnel (2595 metres), opened on 27 February 1964.

Above: In the foreground the Union Steam Ship Company's triple-screw turbine inter-island ferry *Maori* (1907-1944) could carry 600 passengers and served for 37 years.
Below: The *Milburn Carrier II* berths at Lyttelton in 2008.

Above: London Street c1916 has changed little visually in 90 years, but the town has changed with the times. It supports various industries and is an eclectic and vibrant centre with unique and fascinating shops.

Graham Stewart

Central and South Canterbury

1077 P. BEACH ROAD. AKAROA.

Akaroa on Banks Peninsula is where 63 French settlers hoped to claim the South Island for France in 1840, only to find when they arrived in harbour aboard the *Comte de Paris*, escorted by the corvette *L'Aube*, that the British had raised the Union Jack to claim the territory. Akaroa is the oldest colonial town in the South Island and New Zealand's sole French colonial settlement. Akaroa has retained a French flavour with street names of French heritage. In the 1930s it was advertised as the Riviera of Canterbury.

Upper: Regatta Day at Akaroa on New Year's Day 1931 with crowds on the wharf as the inter-island steamer *Maori* comes alongside the jetty on an excursion cruise.

Upper: Beach Road by the harbour is where the French flair delights tourists.

Alexander Turnbull Library, ½040841G

Arthur's Pass was discovered by surveyor Arthur Dudley Dobson in 1864 after whom it was named, and is situated 4 km from the pass on the road between Christchurch and the West Coast. It is at the eastern portal of the 8½ kilometre-long Otira rail tunnel. At 924 metres, it is New Zealand's highest alpine pass.

Above: When Arthur's Pass was the rail terminal from Christchurch: the old railway station where horse-drawn coaches, the only means of travel over the pass, departed for the West Coast.

Below: The modern TranzAlpine express with its picture windows, open-air viewing and buffet carriage, makes the rail journey through the majestic alpine scenery an armchair ride.

Graham Stewart

Collection Christchurch Art Gallery Te Puna o Waiwhetu; purchased 1955   *Courtesy of the Estate of Rita Angus*

'Rita Angus – Cass – 1936': a railway station made famous by New Zealand's most popular painting. The painting is signed 'Rita Cook', a work done by the artist during her brief marriage to Alfred Cook. The station is a request stop when travelling on the TranzAlpine express and is between Craigieburn and Cora Lynn. It was named after Thomas Cass (1817-1895), a pioneer surveyor.

Roy Sinclair

Left: Professional photographer Roy Sinclair captured the Rita Angus scene at Cass as it is today.

Merle Sneddon collection

Rt Hon. Dame Jenny Shipley (1952 -) New Zealand's first woman Prime Minister, December 1997- November 1999. Born Gore 04/02/52; National Party member for Ashburton 1987-1993, for Rakaia 1993-1999; Minister of Social Welfare 1990-1993, Minister of Health 1993-1996, Minister of Women's Affairs 1990-1998, Minister of Transport 1996-1997, Minister of State Services 1996-1997, Minister of State Owned Enterprises, Accident Compensation and in charge of Radio NZ 1996-1997.

Ashburton is one hour's drive, 84 km south-west of Christchurch on the Canterbury Plains by the Ashburton (Hakatare) River. It is a commercial, industrial and market centre for mid-Canterbury farming whose history goes back to the 1850s. The railway line from Christchurch reached Ashburton on 24 August 1874 and continued south to Timaru in February 1876. The town was named in honour of the 2nd Baron Ashburton, a member of the Canterbury Association.

Graham Stewart

Richard William Pearce (1877-1953), pioneer aviator and inventor – was he the first man in the world to achieve powered flight? On 31 March either in 1903 or 1904 his home-made monoplane with a home-made petrol engine and a steerable tricycle undercarriage on pneumatic tyres became airborne. It flew erratically and then veered on to the top of a four- metre-high gorse hedge. There was no way he could have landed on the hedge if he had not been flying. The Wright brothers' first sustained powered flight took place at Kittyhawk, USA, in December 1903. Consensus appears to favour the Wright brothers as no evidence has been able to confirm that the year was 1903 when Pearce first flew. Pearce did achieve a very early powered take-off and is credited with patenting the first aileron in 1907.

Below left: A replica steel model of Richard Pearce's first aeroplane mounted on a pole beside the Main Waitohi Road where the plane came to a sudden stop on top of a gorse hedge in either 1903 or 1904. The plaque at the base reads: 'This monument commemorates the first powered flight to be made by a British citizen in a heavier than air machine. Most evidence indicates this flight took place on 31 March 1903 and ended by crashing on this site.'

Below: Another replica model of Pearce's first aeroplane is part of the Richard Pearce display at the Museum of Transport and Technology at Western Springs, Auckland.

Graham Stewart

Graham Stewart

Jennifer Murray collection

The alpine township of Tekapo is 229 km from Christchurch in South Canterbury at the southern end of Lake Tekapo. It is framed by astonishing landscapes, with the Southern Alps as a backdrop on one side, and sits on the edge of a turquoise-coloured, 20 km, glacial lake with the same name.

Above: The Church of Good Shepherd was built of glacial stones with oak beams and is dedicated as a memorial to the early pioneers of the Mackenzie Country.

Below: A photograph taken during the dedication of the church in August 1935 with the majestic snowy Southern Alps in the background.

Jennifer Murray collection, courtesy Audrey Burtscher

Graham Stewart

The first settler to discover the area was Scotsman James Mackenzie who in 1855 discovered a pass through the mountains which was later named after him. By the 1870s most of the area was divided into large sheep stations.

Right: The sheepdog monument was 'erected by the runholders of the Mackenzie Country and those who also appreciate the value of the Collie dog, without the help of which the grazing of this mountain country would be impossible'. It was unveiled on 7 March 1968 by Governor-General Sir Arthur Porritt.

Graham Stewart

Graham Stewart collection

Above: Foundations of the first Hermitage consisted of blocks of concrete set in kerosene tins and the framework attached to these blocks by No. 8 fencing wire. Construction had started in late 1884, with the 13-room house completed in mid-1885 for the accommodation of about 30 guests. The building was situated near the base of the Mueller Glacier. A new wooden wing was added to this building in 1890; the cob of the original structure had soon crumbled under the severe weather conditions and had to be sheathed with corrugated iron. A further dormitory annexe for 20 beds was completed in 1907, and in April of the same year a telephone line from Fairlie was connected.

On 8 February 1906, at 4 am, two six-horsepower de Dions, after being driven all night from Pukaki through low mist and fording many streams, were the first motorcars to reach the Hermitage. In the same year the Mount Cook Motor Company started running open-air tourers, with only side canvas protection for passengers, to replace the horse-drawn coach service the Mount Cook-Hermitage Company had run from the railhead at Fairlie to the Hermitage since 1886, a journey that had taken two days. By 1914 all the rivers between Fairlie and the Hermitage had been bridged and people were using their own cars.

Courtesy Sir Edmund Hillary Alpine Centre and Museum

Courtesy Sir Edmund Hillary Alpine Centre and Museum

Above: The second Hermitage, a two-storey building with 50 bedrooms, was built at Governors Bush and opened in 1914. In 1922, 22 more rooms were added and hand basins placed in the bedrooms. Two years later a new dormitory wing was built and a hot-water heating system installed.   The second Hermitage was gutted by fire just before 5.30 am on 16 September 1957.

Below: The building of the third Hermitage started on 27 November in the same year, and it opened on 29 May 1958 with accommodation for 60 guests. There have been a number of extensions to the Hermitage since: in 1961 a wing was added to provide 42 more beds; in 1970 a 22-bed extension was completed; in 1975 the Panorama Restaurant; in 1977 the 40-room Wakefield Wing opened; and in 2001 the Aoraki Wing was added.

Courtesy Sir Edmund Hillary Alpine Centre and Museum

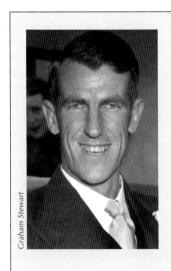

Sir Edmund Hillary (1919-2008): Conqueror of Everest, the world's highest mountain (8850 metres) with Tenzing Norgay on 29 May1953; led New Zealand Antarctic Expedition 1956-1958; using farm tractors completed the first overland journey from Scott Base to the South Pole in January 1958; New Zealand High Commissioner to India 1985-1989; a lifetime of dedication building hospitals and schools in the Himalayas.

Left: Sir Edmund Hillary on his wedding day to Louise Rose (died 1975) at the Diocesan High School chapel, Epsom, Auckland, on 3 September 1953.

Right: A sculpture by Chen Wei-Ming at Orewa, Hibiscus Coast, Auckland, where the parents of Sir Edmund holidayed with their family. Orewa residents place floral tributes, January 2008.

The Sir Edmund Hillary Alpine Centre and Museum at the Hermitage is a tribute to one of the world's greatest explorers and depicts Sir Edmund's close connection with the region where he climbed his first major mountain, achieved a number of impressive first ascents including the difficult south face of Mount Cook, and trained for his Everest and Antarctic expeditions.

Below: The life-size sculpture by Bryn M. Jones of Sir Edmund Hillary at the Sir Edmund Hillary Alpine Centre and Museum at the Hermitage Hotel, Aoraki Mount Cook Percival Village, which he unveiled himself on 5 July 2003.

John Dunlop, courtesy Sir Edmund Hillary Alpine Centre and Museum

Merle Sneddon collection

Surrounded by rolling pastures on the edge of the placid Canterbury Plains, Fairlie is the market and service town for the Mackenzie Country. Behind the town is Burkes Pass which opens to the dramatic Mackenzie Country of tussock wilderness and a rugged mountain scape. It was once an important railway branch line which left the main south line at Washdyke near Timaru. The line opened in January 1884 when the settlement was known as Fairlie Creek and closed in March 1968. A passenger train known as the Fairlie Flyer ran until 1930.

Waimate was first a timber town and is now an inland rural centre at the southern end of the Canterbury Plains at the foot of the rolling Hunters Hills. The first European settler was Michael Studholme in 1864; his descendants still farm land in the area. It was once served by a branch railway line (March 1877-April 1966), and at its peak there were five mixed (passenger and freight) trains a day in each direction, with the haulage of grain and livestock and the inwards supplies of produce. Passenger services ceased in February 1931. Road transport slowly took over all freight cartage, including exports to the port of Timaru. It is known as the centre of the region, being about two hours' drive from Christchurch, Queenstown and Dunedin.

Above and below: The remaining trees in Main Street, Fairlie, were planted as a 1914-1918 First World War Memorial; most of those planted in the Mackenzie Country did not survive the extremes of the climate.

Above and below: Queen Street, Waimate, is a spacious thoroughfare with a collection of Edwardian buildings and a friendly atmosphere.

Graham Stewart

Timaru was first a whaling station in the late 1830s as it was the only place of shelter on the coast. The Maori name Te Maru is said to mean 'the place of shelter'; others maintain the literal meaning of its present form is correct – 'the shady cabbage tree'. In 1859 the ship *Strathallan* arrived with 120 British migrants, and this busy port city has been on a growth pattern ever since. When the artificial harbour was built in the late 1870s (completed 1906) it gave the area an unexpected bonus. The once stony foreshore became a crescent-shaped sandy beach thanks to the sedimentation that drifted across from the new breakwater. The bay was named Caroline Bay after the schooner *Caroline* which collected the whale oil in the 1830s. It is today the largest urban centre in South Canterbury, the hub of the surrounding agricultural and manufacturing district.

The city has a proud heritage – Bob 'Ruby Robert' Fitzsimmons (1863-1917), a blacksmith, was the first triple world champion boxer; it was the birthplace of painter Colin McCahon and poet Allen Curnow; and Phar Lap, regarded as our greatest ever racehorse, was foaled at Seadown, just outside Timaru.

Below: Stafford Street past and present – this street has always been the main street but is now a far more relaxed hub of the city since State Highway One was diverted slightly to the west of the town.
Below left: The junction of Stafford and George Streets looking north.
Below: The intersection of Stafford with Church and Strathallan Streets.

Timaru N. Z.

Graham Stewart collection

Merle Sneddon collection

Jack Lovelock crosses the line to win the 1500 metres at the Berlin Olympic Games in 1936.

John Edward (Jack) Lovelock (1910-1949), medical practitioner and international athlete.
Born Crushington near Reefton; attended Temuka and Fairlie Schools; Timaru Boys' High School; University of Otago; Rhodes Scholar 1931; Exeter College, Oxford, BA 1934, MA 1937; MRCP (London) 1940; World record mile, Princeton USA, 1933; British Empire Games, won the mile 1934; Berlin Olympic Games 1936, won the 1500 metres in 3 minutes 47. 8 seconds, a world record; retired from athletics; served in the RAMC 1939-1945; Manhattan Hospital, New York 1948; killed by train in a New York subway 28 December 1949.

Alexander Turnbull Library, MSX, 2261066

The oak tree presented to Jack Lovelock on 6 August 1936 by Adolf Hitler, after winning the 1500 metres race at the Berlin Olympic Games, continues to grow in the grounds of Timaru Boys' High School.   A plaque in the grounds of the school acknowledges 'A pupil at this school 1924-1928, head prefect and dux 1928'.

Below: Timaru Boys' High School students walk by the historic 'Lovelock' oak tree.

Graham Stewart

All photographs on this page – Graham Stewart

The Bank of Otago building (left), built in 1871, was absorbed by the National Bank in 1875. The former Bank of New South Wales building (right), built in 1883, was strengthened by the Oamaru Borough Council and reopened as the Forrester Gallery in 1983. Both these classic Victorian buildings with grand Corinthian columns were designed by Robert Lawson of Dunedin. The quality of the local limestone (Oamaru stone) has given Oamaru one of the finest 19th century streetscapes in the country.

Otago

Oamaru, a coastal town 115 km north of Dunedin, began humbly in 1853 when runholder Hugh Robison erected a sod hut, a far cry from the structures that would follow with the discovery of the local limestone. Oamaru was an early export port with an open roadstead for frozen meat to the United Kingdom and became a graveyard for many fine vessels.

Above right: The Bank of Otago with the Empire Hotel (est. 1865) on the left in the 1870s.

Below: By the mid-1880s the Bank of New South Wales was standing proudly on Thames Street, slightly overshadowing the building 12 years its senior.

North Otago Museum photograph collection 723

Above: Over 100 years ago tourists enjoyed the experience of sitting and standing on the boulders c1905.

According to Maori folklore, the kai (food)-hinaki (baskets) were washed ashore at Moeraki from the great canoe Arai-te-uru. It was travelling south and foundered in a storm near Matakaea (Shag Point). The cargo of round food baskets and water gourds are Te Kai Hinaki (the Moeraki Boulders); the seed kumara (sweet potatoes) are the irregularly shaped boulders further south.

Graham Stewart

Graham Stewart

Scientists maintain the boulders were once buried in the mudstone cliffs that face the beach. For millions of years the sea has been eroding these cliffs, washing away the soft mudstone that surrounds the boulders, leaving them exposed on the beach. There are still more embedded in the cliffs waiting to be uncovered. The largest boulder is 2.2m in diameter.

About 15 million years ago the mudstone and other rocks were lifted above sea level, and erosion slowly worked away at the new landmass. In time the new coastline was sculptured, exposing the mudstone beds containing the concretions. Concretions are hard masses which form in sedimentary rocks. Their roundness has nothing to do with being washed by the sea – they were round when they formed in the mudstone. They are an intriguing geological phenomenon on the Otago coastline.

Graham Stewart

OLD PORT CHALMERS. NO 23.

Hocken Collections, Uare Taoka o Hakena, University of Otago, E3165/11

Port Chalmers in 1877 – five years after this photograph was taken the first shipment of frozen meat left Port Chalmers in the *Dunedin* for the London market in 1882. The last expedition led by Captain Robert Falcon Scott sailed in the *Terra Nova* from this port for Antarctica on 28 November 1910. The port and township, named after the Rev. Thomas Chalmers, leader of the Free Church of Scotland, is now a large container terminal serving the southern regions of the South Island.

Graham Stewart

Dunedin

James Cook sailed past the entrance to Otago Harbour in 1770 but noted the ocean beaches of St Kilda and St Clair; it is recorded that sealers and whalers first used the harbour in the early years of the 19th century. Three hundred settlers arrived on the ships *John Wickliffe* and *Philip Laing* in March and April 1848 to settle on land purchased from Ngai Tahu which had been subdivided for sale at two pounds an acre. The town was to be called 'New Edinburgh', but consensus won with Dunedin being chosen (Edin on the Hill), Edinburgh's ancient name. It was Edward Gibbon Wakefield of the New Zealand Company who masterminded the establishment of the settlement. Captain William Cargill (1784-1860) and Reverend Thomas Burns (1796-1871), a nephew of the poet Robert Burns, were the founders of the city. The first University in New Zealand was founded in Dunedin in 1869 with the Reverend Thomas Burns its first chancellor.

New Law Courts, Dunedin.

Graham Stewart collection

William Main collection

The old Law Courts building, built on the site of the old gaol on the corner of Castle and Lower Stuart Streets, with a façade of Victorian Gothic design, was claimed at the time to be the cheapest building of its kind in New Zealand when completed in 1902. It balances nicely with the George Troup-designed railway station across the road. On Christmas Eve 1903 City Council electric trams first started rumbling past on their way to the Gardens. Strange as it may seem, this service closed on Christmas Eve 1950.

New Zealand's only castle is Larnach Castle, of Scottish baronial style, on a hilltop on Camp Road on the Otago Peninsula. It was built by banker and politician William Larnach for his first wife, Eliza Jane Guise, a descendant of French nobility. Construction started in 1871 and was not finished until 1887 with the completion of the ballroom. It was three years before the family could move in, and European craftsmen spent another 12 years finishing the interior with the finest of materials from around the world. The castle is now the home of the Barker family who since 1967 has been restoring the 34 rooms and the 14 hectares of gardens.

Graham Stewart

Graham Stewart collection

The Stock Exchange building on Princes Street was built to be the post office but the concept was shelved before it was completed, as it was considered too grand. By 1868 the Otago Museum had moved in, as had the Dunedin School of Art, the first to be established in New Zealand. The University of Otago became the tenant in 1871, and then the building became the New Zealand headquarters for the Colonial Bank and later the Bank of New Zealand. In 1900 the building was purchased by a group of businessmen and became known as the Stock Exchange. The clock came from the 1866 New Zealand Exhibition building. This part of town was the heart of the city for many decades; the building was known by citizens as 'The Exchange'. Sadly, it was demolished in 1969.

Reginald McGovern

DIN, LOOKING NORTH. F.T. Series. No. 752

Graham Stewart collection

For 74 years cable cars carried millions of people up the gradients of High Street, Eglinton Road and Mailer Street to the junction of Parkhill Avenue – from 23 March 1883 until 2 March 1957. The venture was built and operated by a private company, The Mornington Tramway Company Limited. In April 1903 the Mornington Council took over the running of the service, and in 1916 the Dunedin City Corporation Tramways became the operators. Mornington was the last cable car line in Dunedin.

Below: Shades of the most aristocratic of hill slopes in Nob Hill, San Francisco – Mornington cable car No. 101 and trailer No. 109 climb the hill past Grant Street. This ornate home on High Street was first named Threave after Threave House, Kirkcudbright, Solway, Firth, Scotland, but the name did not last. The house was built in 1904 as a retirement home for Watson Shennan, pioneer runholder of Galloway Station, Central Otago.

Graham Stewart

Graham Stewart

Graham Stewart

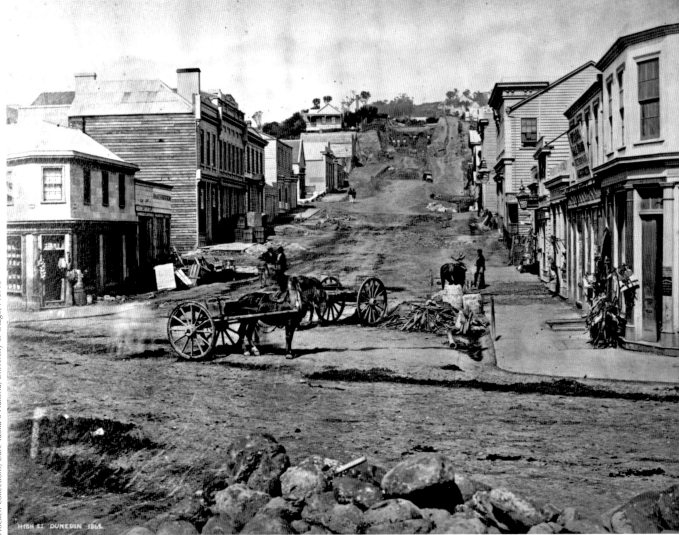

The foot of High Street at Princes Street was the heart of 'The Exchange' area in days of trams, cable cars and later trolley-buses. It was where shoppers coming to town alighted or where people changed from an electric tram to a cable car to visit the hill suburbs.

Above: Looking up High Street in 1862: men can be seen with picks and shovels digging away the roadway to ease the gradient up to Mornington. In true Scottish tradition, the road is built the hard way, straight up the hill; they did not follow the contours of the land, the easy way with sweeping curves.

Reginald McGovern

Above: High Street in the early 1950s with a cable car loading for another trip up the hill.

Facing page, below and right: The Grand Hotel (1883), now the Southern Cross Hotel, has stood on this corner for over 125 years. It has witnessed a passing parade of generations and vehicles from the 10-kilometre-an-hour pace of horse trams, frisky young mares drawing spring carts, sooty steam trams, the distinct clang of the cable car bell, the rattle of electric trams, and the silence of trolley-buses to the vehicles of today.

Graham Stewart

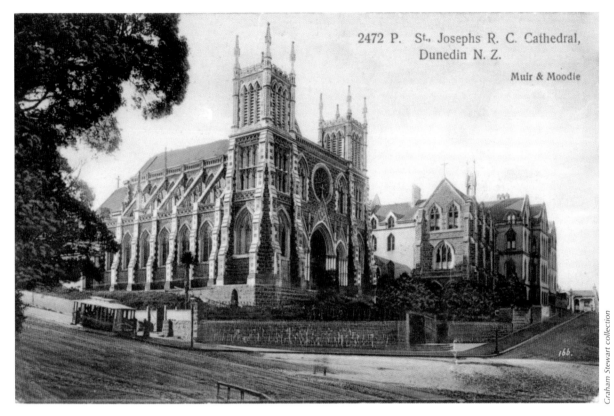

2472 P.   St. Josephs R. C. Cathedral,
Dunedin N. Z.

Muir & Moodie

Graham Stewart collection

St Joseph's Catholic Cathedral looks down on the sweeping curve of Rattray Street, the corner where cable car traction history was made in the 1880s and later adopted in San Francisco. It was young Dunedin-born engineer George Smith Duncan who solved the problem of hauling cable cars around an uphill curve (the grade was 1 in 7½) while still gripping the moving wire cable. Duncan designed the 'pull curve' – a number of small wheels, known as 'drum pulleys', which gently eased the wire rope around the curve and still allowed the car to grip while taking the curve on this hair-raising incline. The service ran from 1881 to 1951. Behind St Joseph's is St Dominic's Priory (1877) in Tennyson Street.

Graham Stewart

Graham Stewart

In 1951 a lunch-time cable car leaves the Arthur Street stop on Rattray Street in the days when many businessmen used the frequent cable car service to travel home for lunch. This pioneer line south of the equator opened in February 1881 and closed in October 1951. Propulsion for the toy-sized trams was provided by an endless cable running in a tunnel beneath the road, this being gripped by an arm hanging down under each car and passing through a slot in a centre rail.

Graham Stewart

Hocken Collections, Uare Taoka o Hakena, University of Otago, F13/9

Above: Looking south down Princes Street in 1861 to where Rattray Street crosses and beyond to High Street on the right. The ghost images of the people are caused by the slow exposure used by the photographer. They would have moved while the photograph was being exposed.

Below left: By 1906 more substantial colonial buildings had replaced the wooden and shingle-roof structures. On the footpaths are gas lamp standards of noble design, while adorning the centre of the roadway are decorative steel centre poles with wrought-iron fancy-work and, perched high above, a 'modern' electric street lamp.

Graham Stewart collection

New Zealand Railway and Locomotive Society collection

Hocken Collections, Uare Taoka o Hakena, University of Otago, E1998/16

The three towers in Lower Stuart Street – the Evening Star, the railway station and the law courts. The railway station is the third structure; the first (1872-1875) was built by the Dunedin and Port Chalmers Railway Company, and in 1875 the Government replaced it with a new station. The third still stands. Opened in November 1907, it was designed by George Troup (mayor of Wellington 1927-1937, knighted 1937).

The Knox Presbyterian Church (1876) iron fence on George Street in the foreground has survived, while buildings around the intersection of London, Pitt and Frederick Streets have fallen. The Royal Albert Hotel (centre right), on the corner of George and London Streets (1864), was first named the Black Bull. The name changed to the Royal Albert in the 1880s to honour Queen Victoria's consort.

Graham Stewart

Alexander Turnbull Library, S.C. Smith, 47633½

The Junction, Roslyn (showing Post Office), Dunedin, N. Z.

Merle Sneddon collection

The Dunedin Technical School was established in 1889, and in 1913 this building on the corner of Stuart Street, where York Place crosses, was built to house the King Edward Technical College. In 1966 it was split into two institutions, the King Edward High School and the Otago Polytechnic. The Kaikorai cable cars (06/10/1900-31/07/1947) were painted blue which was unusual for the era when most public transport vehicles were painted either red or chocolate.

The post office with tower at Highgate in the early 1900s when an electric tram (the first in New Zealand 23/10/1900-31/01/1936) ran from Spylaw Street along Highgate to Ross Street to connect with the Roslyn cable car. Just along the road on the left where the Highgate bridge now crosses Stuart Street, below, was a level-crossing where the Kaikorai cable car line crossed the Maori Hill electric tram line.

Graham Stewart

Alexander Turnbull Library, G4767⅓

The Esplanade on the ocean beach at St Clair is a popular place to promenade in the summer months. The seawall and esplanade opened on 23 April 1913; the cost of the project was borne by the government, the council and the tramways. The tramways paid for a third of the cost as it was felt the improvements would bring people by tram to the beach.

Graham Stewart

Graham Stewart

Yvette Williams (1929-   ): Athlete, first New Zealand woman to win an Olympic gold medal. Born Dunedin 25/04/29. New Zealand championships: shot put (1947-1954); long jump (1948-1954); javelin (1950); discus (1951-1954); 80 metres hurdles (1954). 1950 Empire Games at Auckland: won gold medal for long jump (19 ft 4½ in.), a new games record, silver medal for javelin. 1952 Olympic Games at Helsinki: won long jump, new Olympic record of 20 ft 5½ in. 1954 Empire Games at Vancouver: won shot put with a record distance of 45 ft 9½ in., won discus throw. 20 February 1954 at Gisborne: established a new world record for the long jump of 20 ft 7½ in.

Rona Williams, courtesy Ian Dougherty

Graham Stewart

The upper photograph of Baldwin Street in Dunedin's North East Valley was taken between 1905 and 1910, according to local historians. The street is listed in *The Guinness Book of Records* as the steepest street in the world with a gradient of 1 in 1.266. It has become a popular attraction for local and international visitors. Just down the road the old 1914 North East Valley post office is now a tourist souvenir shop. The street is the venue for a number of annual fun events for runners, and for fund-raising, and in July each year, the world's steepest jaffa race is watched by thousands.

Alexander Turnbull Library, APC, 1190'F

The Taieri Gorge Railway is an award-winning train service which takes tourists from Dunedin into the heartland of Otago through ten tunnels, over a dozen viaducts spanning giant ravines to the spectacular and rugged landscape of Central Otago. The Otago Central railway once ran to Cromwell via Middlemarch, Ranfurly, Omakau, Alexandra and Clyde. The line closed in April 1990, but the section from Dunedin to Middlemarch was sold to Dunedin City and is operated by the Taieri Gorge Railway. The gorge section between Cromwell and Clyde closed in April 1980 for the construction of the Clyde Dam.

> Wingatui is the name William Stevenson gave his farm in 1858. When out shooting he, 'winged a tui'.

Otago

Above: The Wingatui viaduct, built in 1887, is the largest wrought-iron structure in New Zealand. It is 197 metres long and towers 50 metres above Mullocky Creek.

Right: A Taieri Gorge Railway tourist train crosses the Wingatui viaduct.

Stew Robertson

Charles Todd (1868-1942), founder of the largest privately owned family company in New Zealand, The Todd Corporation Ltd. Started a wool-scouring and fellmongery business and acted as stock and station agents in 1885 at Heriot, Formed Todd Motors, a major car, truck and tractor assembler and distributor, Europa Oil, a national petroleum product marketer, Todd Petroleum, oil and gas explorer, producer and marketer. Now, as Todd Energy, incorporating electricity generation, the largest New Zealand-owned energy company. Together with Shell and BP and, latterly, as sole operator, discovered and developed major oil and gas fields in Taranaki, including Kapuni, Maui and Pohokura, played a key role in the development of Clear Communications, now TelstraClear, helped fund and develop Sky Network Television. Other investments include Crown Castle Australia, Landco and Woosh.

Hocken Collections, Uare Taoka o Hakena. University of Otago. E3508/37

Looking from Essex Street to Balclutha on the south bank of the Clutha River. The township was settled upstream from where the river divides into the Matau and Koau branches to surround the island of Inchclutha. Maori knew it as Iwikatea before it became known as Clutha Ferry; then the name Balclutha, a Gaelic name, was chosen by the first Scottish settlers in 1846, the name meaning 'town of the Clyde'. The first bridge over the Clutha River opened in 1868 and was destroyed by floods in 1878. The impressive concrete arch bridge (1935) spans New Zealand's biggest river by volume. State Highway One passes through the centre of this manufacturing and service town for the lower Clutha basin, Otago's southernmost town.

Balclutha and Kaitangata are the gateways to the Catlins Coast: to Kaka Point, Nugget Point, Owaka, Tahakopa Bay, through the Catlins Forest Park to Porpoise Bay, Curio Bay and Waipapa Point.

Graham Stewart

The village of Kaitangata on the Matau branch of the Clutha River was where the Kaitangata Railway and Coal Company mined for over 80 years with their own railway line to Stirling and their own fleet of steam locomotives. The first coal was railed to Dunedin on 19 June 1876. Diminishing returns from the company's collieries saw closure in October 1959. When the Mines Department took over the 5.95 km private line in 1956, it was the oldest privately owned railway in the country. The line was finally closed on 30 December 1970.

Above: The steam locomotive with a rake of coal wagons, moving along Eddystone Street past the post office and a local store in July 1955, was built for the coal company in Glasgow to the same design as the Government D-class locomotives.

Hocken Collections, Uare Taoka o Hakena, University of Otago, E5922/26A

Motorists travelling south on the 44 km 'Presidential Highway', as State Highway One between Clinton and Gore is now called, would be surprised to know the township of Clinton was once an important railway centre. An early station complex with refreshment rooms and a post office was burnt down in the mid-1890s, and replaced by the station with six chimney tops in the photograph, showing staff standing in line. Today it is only a whistle-stop with an elf-sized station building about half the size of the original railway public toilets.

Graham Stewart

Graham Stewart

Central Otago

Central Otago in mid-winter – Highway 85. Turn right to St Bathans, the old gold town, and Blue Lake.

D. L. A. Turner

Above: The Poolburn viaduct in the days of regular railcar services between Dunedin and Alexandra. The Sunday afternoon railcar from Dunedin to Alexandra, RM 53, in January 1971.

Right: Stone for the piers of the Poolburn viaduct was cut from rock outcrops on the hill in the distance and carted to the site by horse and drays. Work commenced in early 1901 on the bridge and the line was officially opened on 29 November 1904.

Olsen and Hardwicke Knight, Otago Cavalcade

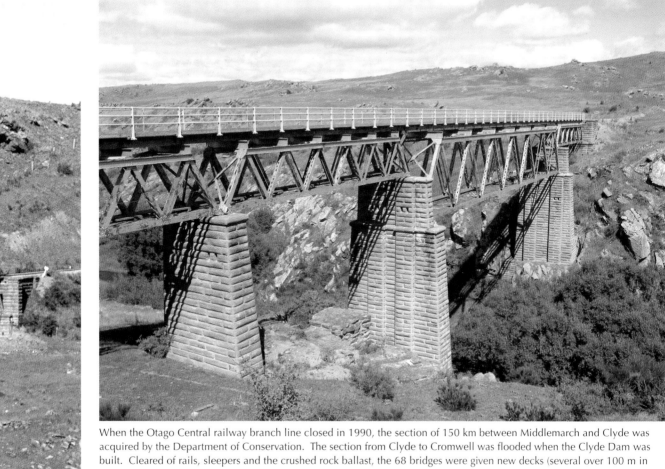

Stew Robertson

When the Otago Central railway branch line closed in 1990, the section of 150 km between Middlemarch and Clyde was acquired by the Department of Conservation. The section from Clyde to Cromwell was flooded when the Clyde Dam was built. Cleared of rails, sleepers and the crushed rock ballast, the 68 bridges were given new decks (several over 100 m in length) and fitted with hand rails. In February 2000 the Otago Central Rail Trail through the Maniototo Plains was opened for walkers and bikers. Tourists can travel in either direction and leave the trail where it crosses a public road. Mountain bikers allow three to five days and walkers five to seven days. There are plenty of refreshment and accommodation stops along the trail, which has become a year-round recreational attraction.

Below: A Cromwell-to-Dunedin passenger train crosses the Manuherikia River
viaduct near Lauder, hauled by a Q class locomotive on 30 December 1936.

Otago Settlers Museum, S. A. Rockliff collection

Stew Robertson

Above: Wedderburn from the road-rail crossing in 1972 when trains were still passing through the settlement. It was once a coaching stage on the road to Dunstan and was the highest altitude railway station in Otago and Southland.

Below: Like an egg tempera canvas by Grahame Sydney: The artist's painting 'July in Maniototo' 1975, of this railway goods shed at Wedderburn, has made this part of the country a must see for visitors to the Maniototo.

Hocken Collections, Uare Taoka o Hakena, University of Otago, E5377/32

St Bathans is on a 30 km loop road off State Highway 85. It once had 2000 residents at the height of the gold-rush and 13 hotels where they relaxed. Only one hotel remains, the sun-dried brick building, the Vulcan Hotel, built during the first rush in 1869. You can count the number of permanent residents on your fingers and toes these days. Close by is the 'blue lake', a hole left following the gold-sluicing in the 1880s.

Graham Stewart

Hocken Collections, Uare Taoka o Hakena, University of Otago, 169/3/a

Alexandra's old elegant suspension bridge took three years to build and was opened in June 1882. The bridge was 165.6m in length; it had a deck supported by four cables on each side. The cables were supported by two piers. Constructing two concrete foundations below river level inside a coffer-dam in a wild and powerful river was a high-risk task in the 1880s. The piers of the old bridge remain. The present bridge was opened in July 1958.

Donald Lamont

Alexander Turnbull Library, 019560

Hocken Collections, Uare Taoka o Hakena, University of Otago, E2233/22

Clyde is on the banks of the Clutha River, downstream from the mighty Clyde hydro-electric dam (1990), New Zealand's third largest capacity hydro power station. It was the centre of the Dunstan goldfields in the 1860s and was known as Dunstan in those golden days.

Right: On the corner of Sutherland and Matau Streets is the Dunstan Hotel (c1865), built of local stone. The first charabanc coach belonged to Craig and Company.

Below: Further north down Sutherland Street is Dunstan House Clyde (1880s), also a local stone structure, which was built on the site of its predecessor (1863). Both hotels still offer hospitality.

Donald Lamont

Donald Lamont

Valentine, Graham Stewart collection

Cromwell is New Zealand's furthermost inland town and, like other settlements in the district, came alive with the gold-rush in 1862. It was first known as 'the Junction' because of its position at the fork of the Kawarau and Clutha Rivers. Old Cromwell town is the reincarnation of buildings that were moved when part of the town, including the old bridge (1865), was submerged into Lake Dunstan when the Clyde Dam was built in 1990. The town today is the centre of the stone-fruit growing district.

Donald Lamont

Gladys M. Goodall, Laurence Eagle collection

Wanaka on the southern shore of Lake Wanaka, the once small tourist country town that serves the surrounding farms and the back-country sheep and cattle stations, is now the fastest-growing resort town in Central Otago and is the front door to the Haast Pass and Mount Aspiring National Park. Looming overhead across the lake is Mount Roy from where there is a 360- degree stunning panoramic view of the Alpine region. The 'Warbirds over Wanaka' air show, held every second year at Easter, features historic fighter planes and always brings thousands to the town.

Simon Darby, Alpine Image

The first Maori settlements on the shores of Lake Wanaka were razed to the ground by a northern Maori war raid in 1836. By 1858 Europeans had ventured into the area, had claimed tracts of land and stocked them with cattle and sheep. Tourism arrived in 1881 with the launch of a paddle-steamer to take sightseers to the head of the lake. It has since become an all-year-round tourist town with swimming and boating at the lake in summer and skiing in the winter months.

Gladys M. Goodall, Laurence Eagle collection

Simon Darby, Alpine Image

Courtesy Peter and Vicki Byrne

Above left: The Spanish-style, 56-bed Wanaka Hotel was destroyed by fire in June 1958 and was replaced by a luxury Tourist Hotel Corporation hotel (*above right*) which has been enlarged and modernised over the years.

Left and below: The Cardrona Hotel is a New Zealand icon and has been around since the gold-mining days in the early 1860s when it was a boisterous meeting place for gold-diggers. It is on the Crown Range Road near the turn-off to the Waiorau Snow Farm. Behind the historic façade is spacious accommodation together with a restaurant and bar that open out onto a garden dining and wining area. The ski fields in the surrounding area are Cardrona; Treble Cone, the South Island's largest ski field; the Waiorau Snow Farm for cross-country skiers and the nearby Snow Park, a popular playground for snow-boarders and freestylers.

Queenstown and Lakes District

Hocken Collections, Uare Taoka o Hakena, University of Otago, E1843/31

Simon Crawford collection

Lake Wakatipu. Queenstown. F.G.R. 6391.

Arrowtown has kept much of the gold-rush atmosphere of the 1860s with many of the original wooden and stone 19th century buildings still standing and now used as shops and restaurants. The privately owned miners' cottages on Buckingham Street nestle beneath old sycamore trees which turn the town into a forest of red and gold colour tones each autumn.

Above: The paddle-steamer *Antrim* (1868) at the steamer wharf at Queenstown carried locals and tourists for over 50 years on Lake Wakatipu.

Below: Today the 'Lady of the Lake', the twin-screw steamer *Earnslaw* built in 1912, is only a few years off celebrating 100 years of service. The New Zealand Government Railways purchased the service from the Lake Wakatipu Shipping Company in 1902.

Graham Stewart

Ballarat Street, and Eichardt's Hotel, Queenstown, N. Z.

Alexander Turnbull Library, PAcoll 748960

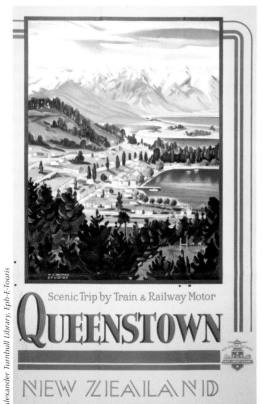

Scenic Trip by Train & Railway Motor

QUEENSTOWN

NEW ZEALAND

Alexander Turnbull Library, Eph-E-Touris

The opulent Eichardt's Hotel (1870s) on the Mall in Ballarat Street looks out on the charming lakeside setting over Lake Wakatipu to the Remarkables and the Eyre Mountains. The settlement was first used by sheep drovers in the late 1850s and was then known as 'The Camp' where pioneer runholder William Rees built a cottage in the early 1860s; then came the gold-mining years when the town sprang to life. In 1863 residents gave the town its name, said to be after Queenstown in Ireland; others maintain it was such an idyllic setting that it was a place 'fit for a Queen', so it was named in honour of Queen Victoria.

Graham Stewart

The Cromwell coach, drawn by four horses, prepares to leave Eichardt's Hotel on Ballarat Street in the 1870s. In October 1878 the downtown area of Queenstown suffered severe flooding, and folklore has it that a barman at Eichardt's continued to serve drinks while up to his waist in water. A brass tablet on the waterfront marks the level of this record flood. In 1999 three-quarters of the town was flooded by rising water from the lake, a threat that no longer exists.

Lake Wakatipu is crossed by the forty-fifth parallel of latitude – being halfway between the South Pole and the equator.

Right: The paddle-steamer *Mountaineer* leaves the old ferry jetty at the foot of Ballarat Street.

Below: The fleet's in! The steamers (from left) *Earnslaw* (1912 -   ), *Mountaineer* (1872-1932) and *Ben Lomond* (1872-1951). The *Earnslaw* has a Historic Places Trust classification and consequently the vessel is a protected part of New Zealand's heritage. The foreshore of Queenstown c1915 with hardly a building in sight is in contrast to Queenstown today (*facing page*).

Simon Crawford collection

The "Mountaineer" leaving Queenstown. N.Z. 846. F.G.R.

Simon Crawford collection

Left: The vintage TSS *Earnslaw* steams out of Queenstown Bay on an excursion to Walter Peak high-country farm.

The TSS *Earnslaw* was built in Dunedin. The hull, with all the plates and frames numbered, was bolted together in the builder's yard in Dunedin, then dismantled and all the materials railed by special goods train to Kingston where it was erected near a slipway.

Queenstown is the hub for a wide range of attractions from bungy-jumping, hang-gliding, skiing Coronet Peak, rafting, jet-boating, horse treks and farm excursions, to wilderness adventures.

Graham Stewart

Graham Stewart

The spectacular Skippers Canyon Road would be the most terrifying and inhospitable road in the country, so much so that rental car operators do not allow you to drive their vehicles over the road. Carved from schist rock, this 22 km road winds through the river gorge with rock formations towering overhead. The Skippers swing- bridge is 90 metres above the Shotover River bed. The best way to experience this rugged part of the country is to take a scenic four-wheel-drive safari experience and see firsthand in a relaxed manner the gold-mining history of the area.

Below: Skippers Canyon Jet of Queenstown uses specifically designed 4WD vehicles for the rough terrain with 13 seats plus the driver elevated for the view down off the road edge into the canyon.

Graham Stewart collection

The Skippers, Wakatipu, N. Z.

Simon Crawford collection

Skippers Canyon Jet, Queentown

Hocken Collections, Uare Taoka o Hakena, University of Otago, E6192/28

Above: Looking south to Kingston on what is State Highway Six today, with the notorious Devil's Staircase just ahead in the days when it was a rough metal road with little room to pass and clouds of dust. The other devil on the New Zealand road network is between Wairoa and Napier in Hawke's Bay. It winds its way down several hundred metres of hillside in under a kilometre and up again and is known as the 'Devil's Elbow'.

Graham Stewart

Left: Driving south from Queenstown to Kingston hugging the eastern shore of Lake Wakatipu on State Highway Six, is now a relaxing and pleasant experience with fabulous scenic vistas all the way.

Kingston, like many settlements, was once a Maori village at the southern end of Lake Wakatipu. It was formerly the terminus of the branch railway line from Gore which connected with Lake Wakatipu ferry services. The line opened in July 1878, and passenger services closed in October 1937, apart from special excursion trains. In December 1971 the Kingston Flyer tourist train service started running 61 km to Lumsden. The tourist train now only runs to Fairlight, a distance of 14 km, in the holiday season from 1 October to 30 April, using restored steam locomotives Ab 778 and 795, with wooden steam-heated carriages, some dating back to 1898.

Left: Railway and ferry jetty 1890s.
Below: Steam locomotive Ab 778 (1925) on the turntable at Kingston and the TSS *Earnslaw* at the ferry jetty in the summer of 1972.

Alexander Turnbull Library, ½028781F

D.A.L.Turner

New Zealand Herald

Murray Lloyd

The original Te Anau Hotel was built in 1890 and was purchased in 1906 by the Department of Tourist and Health Resorts. Over the years the hotel was enlarged and upgraded (1907, 1926, 1944 and 1947). In 1957 the Tourist Hotel Corporation took over and more rooms were added, but in 1965 the old hotel (*above*) was destroyed by fire.

Below: Today's Te Anau Hotel and Villas was opened in November 1966. The Te Anau glow-worm caves are on the western shore of the lake.

Murray Lloyd

Alexander Turnbull Library, ½024836F

The road to Milford Sound, which pierces the main divide at the head of the Hollyford Valley through the rough-hewn rock tunnel with a gradient of one to ten sloping down to the Milford side, is an experience in itself. Excavation started in 1935 and the tunnel was pierced in 1940. On 17 March 1940 the first party from the Milford Hotel walked through the tunnel. Construction work stopped during the Second World War, and in 1945 a large avalanche severely damaged the eastern tunnel portal. Three men were killed during construction. The tunnel is 1.2 km in length and was named after Harry Homer who discovered the saddle in 1889; it was opened for traffic in 1953.

Gladys M. Goodall, Laurence Eagle collection

Fiordland

Graham Stewart collection

Real Journeys, RJ66

From the Homer tunnel it is 18 km to Milford Sound, a journey that starts through sheer rock walls which can be a curtain of waterfalls in the winter season. The first glimpse of the incredibly grand Mitre Peak, one of New Zealand's best-known scenic icons, is an amazing, inspiring sight. Fiordland, in the south-west corner of the South Island, is unsurpassed in beauty and the sheer magnitude of the landscapes. In 1986 it was judged as having 'superlative natural phenomena' and 'outstanding examples of....the earth's evolutionary history' when it was made a World Heritage area.

Alexander Turnbull Library, Eph-A-Tourism-Milford-1935

Milford Sound is an incredibly grand fiord with Mitre Peak (1692 metres) standing majestically to dominate the skyline. Maori knew the sound as Piopio-tahi 'a single thrush'; it was renamed, according to folklore, by sealer Captain John Grono (1820s) after Milford Haven in Wales. Captain Stokes of the survey ship *Acheron* (1851) is said to have named Mitre Peak because of the shape's resemblance to a bishop's mitre or head-dress when viewed from the south. The sound is best viewed from a launch; the sheer granite towering cliffs reach into the sky and plunge into the fiord; the thundering Bowen Falls hurtle 165 metres. Then there are the Stirling Falls further down the sound and the seal colonies. The length of the fiord is approximately 16 km to the Tasman Sea. It has been a favourite place for overseas cruise ships to visit, bringing passengers ashore in the ships' boats. In the 1930s it was a busy port of call for cruise ships from Melbourne. Pioneers in air travel to Milford included Mr Bradshaw of Southland who made three successful landings in 1939, and on 16 July 1939 Captain Mercer (Air Travel NZ) landed on the beach at Deep Water Basin.

The London *Spectator* in 1908 ran the headline ' The Finest Walk in the World' to describe the Milford Track, a 53.9 km walk that takes four to five days from Milford to Lake Te Anau. It involves boat travel at both ends and traverses some spectacularly beautiful scenery.

Alexander Turnbull Library, 037795

Milford Sound N.Z.

Alexander Turnbull Library, 062455

Real Journeys, RJ63

5307. SUTHERLAND'S ACCOMMODATION HOUSE, MILFORD SOUND N.Z.   Muir & Moodie
THE FINEST SCENERY IN THE WORLD IS ON THE "MILFORD-TE ANAU" OVERLAND ROUTE.

Graham Stewart collection

MITRE PEAK AND HOTEL, MILFORD SOUND. N.Z   G.B.S. 24

Graham Stewart collection

Accommodation began with huts and later accommodation houses, as they were called, like Sutherland's Accommodation House (*above left*). Donald Sutherland built three huts in 1878, naming them 'The City of Milford'. The famous Sutherland Falls, at 630 metres the highest in New Zealand, are an everlasting memorial to this man. The first hotel opened in December 1928 and was rebuilt and remodelled over the years. Fire over time has been a demon in the sound: in February 1950 the east wing of the hotel was destroyed and in 1959 another fire, which started in the kitchen, burnt the centre of the building to the ground.

The Manapouri-Doubtful Sound Tourist Company's first hostel at Deep Cove by the mouth of the Lyvia River and the launch *Constance* which took visitors on a tour of the sounds in the 1950s.

Captain John Grono on the *Governor Bligh* entered Doubtful Sound in January 1810. A Welshman, he was the first European to explore the sound fully. He named Elizabeth Island at the head of the sound after his wife, Elizabeth Bristowe.

Real Journeys

Weekly News, Graham Stewart

The tourist launch *Constance* in Deep Cove during the winter of 1956. In the background is Wilmot Pass, a narrow saddle between Mount Wilmot on the right and a chain of mountains on the left.

Doubtful Sound at 421 metres is the deepest of the fiords; it is long and winding with three arms between Deep Cove and the open sea, a distance of over 40 km. It is three times longer than Milford Sound. Cook sighted the entrance in 1770 and called it Doubtful Harbour. The arms of Doubtful Sound protrude deep into the heart of Fiordland National Park, within the Te Wahipounamu World Heritage area. The sound is reached by boat across Lake Manapouri, then a bus trip over the rugged Wilmot Pass (670.9 metres).

The story of opening Doubtful Sound to tourism is one of enthusiasm and dedication by a young couple from Invercargill, Les and Olive Hutchins, who bought the rights to the track crossing Wilmot Pass, two small and rather aged boats and a dilapidated hut at Deep Cove. They named their venture the Manapouri-Doubtful Sound Tourist Company, and in the summer of 1954 began taking visitors on guided walking tours to what was then one of the wildest and most remote areas in the world. Regular transport services were non-existent, supplies were hundreds of miles away and 'tourists' were a scarce commodity in those days. There was no road into the sound. It is thanks to their vision and determination in those pioneering days that today the spectacular beauty of this area of Fiordland can be shared with visitors from around the world.

Real Journeys, RJ23

DOUBTFUL SOUND FROM WILMOT PASS, N.Z.

Pictorial Publications, William Main collection

Tourists wishing to explore Doubtful Sound before the road was built had to be fit and keen to tackle the walking track up and over Wilmot Pass and down into the sound. The pass was discovered by surveyor E.H. Wilmot. The road connecting the West Arm of Lake Manapouri to Deep Cove was built in the 1960s to carry materials into the construction of the underground power station at West Arm and since then has been a bonus for tourists visiting the area. The view from the summit of Wilmot Pass gives an exceptional vista of remote wonderland.

Left: A tour bus on the Wilmot Pass Road in the late 1960s.
Below: In 2004 a tour bus is stopped at the summit to give people the opportunity to photograph and admire the view of the sound.

Real Journeys

Southland

Leo White, New Zealand Herald

Simon Crawford collection

Gore, 68 km north-east of Invercargill on the banks of the Mataura River in central Southland, is the shopping centre for the farming community and was once the junction for several branch railway lines, including the branch line to Kingston via Lumsden which opened on 31 July 1880. Gore is famous for Hokonui moonshine whisky made by Scottish settlers in illicit stills in the Hokonui hills from the mid-19th century. It flourished from the days of prohibition to just before the Second World War. Their home-made fiery spirits are now part of the region's folklore. It is also famous for brown trout fishing and as a country and western town which hosts the annual Gold Guitar Awards, a ten-day festival.

Above: The old Gore post office, now denuded of its tower, was a striking brick structure when built. It is now home to a florist, bakery and café and, upstairs, the Art South Gallery of Fine Art.

Mataura by the river of the same name attracts fishermen from Japan and the USA with some of the best dry-fly trout fishing to be found. It is the best 'match the hatch' fishing in the country. 8 km south at Tuturau was where the last tribal wars were fought in 1836 when Southland Maori defeated invaders from the north. Te Puoho and his Ngati Toa warriors had marched from Nelson via Westland and over the Haast Pass to surprise Southland's Ngai Tahu from the rear.

Above and below: Mataura town bridges old and new. The 'new' bridge was opened by the Minister of Public Works, the Hon. Robert Semple, on 22 July 1939.

Graham Stewart

Merle Sneddon collection

Hocken Collections, Uare Taoka o Hakena, University of Otago, E5098/7A

Winton and the nearby stream were named after stockman Thomas Winton of the 1850s; in 1863 native bush was cleared to make the Great North Road as diggers trekked north to the goldfields. The town mushroomed when it became the terminus for the first section of the Invercargill-to-Kingston railway line in 1871. In 1895 the town was shocked when Minnie Dean was found guilty of child murder and was hanged, but was proud when in 1919 Winton appointed the first woman town clerk in New Zealand. Miss Ivy Russell held the position for 35 years.

Above: Traffic on the Great North Road in the early 1930s raises the dust as the cars motor through town at a good pace. The Winton Hotel was established in 1889.

Riverton on the estuary of the Aparima River, 38 km west of Invercargill, claims to be the South Island's oldest European settlement, dating back to the sealing and whaling days. In the late 1790s the first European seal-hunters had arrived in Southland from the Australian colony of Sydney. The frontier town of Jacob's River (a nickname given a Maori chief by whalers), as it was then known, was established by Captain John Howell c1836. Howell later married the daughter of a Maori chief and acquired land holdings through his Maori family connections. The locals say with a smile that the area is the 'Riviera of the South'.

Graham Stewart

Invercargill is New Zealand's southernmost city, 217 km south-west of Dunedin. The name was derived from 'Inver' for the meeting of the two waters (Oreti and Makarewa Rivers) and 'Cargill' after Captain William Cargill, superintendent of Otago. John Thomson, the surveyor who planned the city, named all the main streets after Scottish rivers: Dee, Esk, Forth, Tay and Yarrow. Blessed with wide thoroughfares, American servicemen facetiously claimed during the Second World War that the trams would have been more profitable had they run across the streets instead of along them.

Streets on the level and of regal width were ideal for horse-drawn trams, the first making its maiden trip to Gladstone in December 1881. In December 1883 the service was extended along Tay and Conon Streets to Ettrick Street and along East Road to Mary Street. An extension to Biggar Street along Conon Street and to Waikiwi was completed in 1884. The horse cars ground to a halt in March 1908 after a fire destroyed the stables, tram barn and four trams.

Graham Stewart collection

Graham Stewart

Graham Stewart collection

The City Council installed an electric tramway system to North and South Invercargill, Waikiwi and Georgetown, which started with fanfare and free rides on 26 March 1912. The last remaining service was to North Invercargill which closed with thousands packing Dee Street for a final farewell on 10 September 1952. The *Southland Daily News* reported that Invercargill had never seen anything like it since VE and VJ Day celebrations.

Facing page top: On Dee Street is the old post office (1890s) with Hansom cabs and a tram waiting for fares c1914. On the old town Civic Square is the band rotunda (behind the tram, see also page 313) which had opened on 15 February 1893. From the band rotunda troops were farewelled off to war and welcomed home, band concerts were held and it was where crowds gathered for historic occasions.

Facing page lower: The Troopers' Memorial was erected in 1907 to remember those who served in the South African Boer War. It stands like a sentry at the junction of Dee and Tay Streets and The Crescent. Behind the memorial is the Bank of New Zealand, one of many classic buildings to grace this intersection.

Above right: The new post office on Dee Street was opened on 28 July 1941. Opposite the post office (now the Quest Hotel serviced apartments) and the Majestic Theatre building (where the Reading Cinema is now), was the starting point of the city tram services which ran for 40 years.

Graham Stewart

Graham Stewart

Graham Stewart

Below: A tram leaves the southernmost electric tram terminus in the world by St Andrew's Presbyterian Church in September 1951 for the city. The terminus was where Ellis Road meets Tramway Road, just before the old railway level-crossing of the Invercargill-Tokanui line.

Left: The days of trams and steam trains have long gone, but the local pub down the road, the Southland Tavern, has commemorated the era with the name of a bar.

Graham Stewart

Merle Sneddon collection

Bluff is New Zealand's southernmost town and port, 26 km south of Invercargill on a peninsula extending out into Foveaux Strait. It is one of the country's oldest European towns, having been settled continuously since 1824, when it was first home to sealers, whalers and flax merchants. The first record of a ship entering Bluff Harbour was in 1813 when the *Perseverance* visited from Sydney. In 1856 the settlement was named Campbelltown, but the harbour retained the name Bluff. On 1 April 1917 the official name became Bluff. A famous 'son' is Sir Joseph Ward (1856-1930) who received some of his education at the local state school; he served on the Campbelltown Borough Council, was mayor (1881-1886, 1897-1898), chairman of the Bluff Harbour Board (1883-1888, 1893-1894), prime minister (1906-1912, 1928-1930), KCMG 1901, GCMG 1930.

Above: Gore Street with the post office on the corner of Lee Street (now the Bluff Lodge) and beyond the club at Bluff Hotel. Sir Joseph Ward's mother, Hannah, was a publican in the town and Joseph married a local publican's daughter, Teresa De Smidt, in December 1883.

Graham Stewart

The South Port Island harbour of 40 ha, an immense man-made artificial land mass reclaimed from the sea using dredging as a backfill, was opened on 3 June 1960. Bluff is home to the Tiwai Point aluminium smelter at Tiwai Point (opened 1971); the smelter is powered from the Lake Manapouri underground power station. It is also the home of the famous Bluff oyster (ostrea lutaria) dredged from Foveaux Strait and one of the world's finest according to gourmets. The Oyster Bay Bluff Oyster and Southland Seafood Festival is held in April each year.

Graham Stewart

From Cape Reinga to Bluff, via the Bay of Islands, the Hokianga, Auckland, Coromandel, Waikato, King Country, Central Plateau, Bay of Plenty, East Cape, Hawke's Bay, Taranaki, Manawatu, Wairarapa, Wellington, Nelson, Marlborough, Westland, Canterbury, Otago, Fiordland and Southland. My wife, Anne, was my map reader – the lady navigator over many thousands of kilometres we travelled together to make this book a reality. Anne is wearing Wellington colours at the end of the road at Stirling Point, Bluff, which match perfectly with the Automobile Association colours on the signpost above.

Below: Stirling Point, 1.5 km south of Bluff and the southern terminus of State Highway One, is named after William Stirling who arrived at Bluff in 1836 and managed the whaling station once situated at this point. He purchased this land from Tuhawaiki, a Maori chief who was known as 'bloody Jack' to Europeans because he had learnt his English from rough whalers and sealers and used the word bloody a lot. Stirling died from consumption in 1851, said to have been due to the 'inclemency of the elements while prosecuting the masters of the deep'. Stirling's whaling station became the pilot station at Bluff.

Graham Stewart

Merle Sneddon collection

Above: Looking along Elgin Terrace, Oban, to the old Oban Hotel (now the South Sea Hotel) on the foreshore of Halfmoon Bay c1920s. The hotel was not granted a liquor license until 1952; the first bar opened in 1955. The dog in the foreground has long since met his maker, but the dog in the recent photograph (*below*) could be a descendant at first glance! The dog is a Labradoodle named Dash, owned by Di Morris and Pete Bayne who are residents on the island.

Murray Lloyd

Stewart Island

Stewart Island is only 20 minutes by plane from Invercargill or one hour by catamaran ferry from Bluff across Foveaux Strait (32 km) to the settlement of Oban in Halfmoon Bay, the main settlement on the island. The island was named after the first officer of the *Pegasus* from Port Jackson, Australia, who while on a sealing expedition in 1809 began charting the southern coasts. The Maori name for the island, Te Punga o Te Waka a Maui, translated means' the anchor stone of Maui's canoe'. It refers to the part played by this island in the legend of Maui and his crew, who from their canoe (the South Island) caught and raised the great fish, the North Island. Rakiura is the more commonly used Maori name today, meaning 'Glowing Skies', and is the name of the island's national park. The first Europeans were whalers who arrived in the 1830s. The island's Rakiura National Park is a haven for bush walks, native bird life, hunting for Virginian whitetail deer, fishing for blue cod and diving. Kiwi outnumber humans: it is estimated there are 20,000 Stewart Island brown kiwis there.

Merle Sneddon collection

Above: The township of Oban in Halfmoon Bay with the ferry and fishing jetty in the distance.

Murray Lloyd

Gladys M. Goodall, Laurence Eagle collection

Before 1877 there was no ferry service. All masters of vessels heading for Stewart Island had to call at the Bluff post office to obtain a clearance and would be handed a bag of mail, stores and the occasional passengers. The first ferry was the *Ulva* with other cutters relieving; the Bluff Harbour Board's first tug, the paddle-steamer *Awarua,* served from 1885 to 1889, followed by the *Theresa Ward* (1900) and the *Southland* (1927). In 1930 the *Awarua* (ex *Tamatea*) maintained the run until called to war service in 1942. The first *Wairua,* a steamer converted to diesel in 1947, served from December 1944 to June 1959. The Westport tug *James O'Brien* and the old lighthouse steamer *Matai* were then used until the first purpose-built ferry, the new *Wairau* (*left*) was commissioned in 1961. It was built with stabilizers and licensed to carry 287 passengers. The *Wairau* was withdrawn in the mid-1980s due to rising costs and the opening of the island's airport. Amphibians now cross in one hour.

Gladys M. Goodall, Laurence Eagle collection

Above: The island was served for a number of years, starting on 1 October 1950, by Grumman Widgeon seaplanes, good for those with means. They would land in the bay, taxi to the beach, run up onto the sand in front of the Oban Hotel and turn around to face the sea. It was then just a matter of lugging your luggage up the beach.

Stewart Island Flights now fly daily services from Invercargill to the airstrip on the island at Ryan's Creek, a 20-minute flight.

Murray Lloyd

Author Postscript

I started travelling New Zealand roads when tarseal was a bonus. As a youngster in 1940 my first adventure was with family driving from Auckland to Lake Waikaremoana – fording many streams, being piggy-backed 'ashore' when the car got stuck in the middle of a swift-flowing stream – then on to Napier where earthquake damage was still visible, and home across the Taupo Road, a mammoth challenge in those years.

In those years riding in charabanc-type motor-buses to Matakohe and Whangarei for school holidays seemed never-ending journeys, the continual double declutching of gears over hilly, twisting and dusty unsealed roads. The horse 'Peggy' I rode as a youngster features on page 41. I experienced travelling by train in smoky, upright, second-class carriages and the luxury of overnight sleeper comfort when working for a newspaper meant first-class privileges on the North Island main trunk. Covering the Royal Tours of the 1950s, I worked with pioneer photographers W.B. (Bill) Beattie of *Weekly News* fame, Tudor Collins of kauri fame and Leo White of aviation fame.

Flying under the central span of the Auckland Harbour Bridge in the co-pilot's seat with pilot Freddie Ladd in a Grumman Widgeon amphibian aircraft before the bridge opened did not amuse the authorities. Flying in formation in an open-cockpit Tiger Moth with a leather flying helmet firmly strapped to the head, slightly behind a Fletcher topdressing aircraft to capture on film the spread of fertilizer over pastures in the Otorohanga district when aerial topdressing was in its infancy; flying at low altitude around the Southern Alps in mid-winter in a single-prop Auster aircraft with Second World War ace Popeye Lucas of Cecil Peak Station, Queenstown; covering the building of hydro-electric power stations on the Waikato, Maraetai, and Whakamaru, and the first geo-thermal power tests at Wairakei, Taupo; crossing the Mohaka River on the Taupo Road during the building of the road bridge in a self-propelled flying-fox chair which seemed like being in outer space in the early 1960s; a fast drive on Christmas Day 1953 from Auckland to cover the tragic Tangiwai railway disaster. In the top photograph on page 118, I am the person half-crouched with my back to the camera at left, standing on one of the bridge girders, taking a photograph at Tangiwai – all unforgetable experiences.

I travelled by inter-island ferry between Wellington and Lyttelton when the weather always seemed far from kind and the standard morning cup of tea with a slice of white buttered bread was delivered to your cabin by a Union Steamship Company steward at daybreak, then waiting for the car to be unloaded in a rope sling by the ship's crane.

I have memories of being snowbound at Arthur's Pass when the only sound apart from the arrival and departure of a steam train was the jangling of the snow chains on Oscar Coberg's vintage Rolls Royce taxi through the middle of the township; flying in twin-wing de Havilland DH89 Rapides to West Coast destinations; being introduced to an eccentric old man in Wildberry Street, Woolston, by the name of Richard Pearce, not knowing, as some still insist, that he was the first man in the world to achieve powered flight – worse still, not taking his photograph!

I tramped into Doubtful Sound in the winter of 1956 over the Wilmot Pass before road access with Les Hutchins, the founder of the Manapouri-Doubtful Sound Tourist Company. I witnessed the building of the Benmore Dam on the Waitaki River, walking beside pit ponies hauling rakes of coal wagons into the underground mine at the old coal-mining town of Kaitangata out from Balclutha and arriving at nightfall on the express at Invercargill to catch a tram into the unknown to the South Invercargill Trust Hotel.

And still more journeys: on the ferry *Wairau* (1944-1959) as a guest of Captain Ian Williams, feeling uncomfortable in the turbulent waters of Foveaux Strait to Stewart Island. Staying at the Oban Hotel on the island (the bar had only been opened a year) when police made a surprise visit to check on six o'clock closing and arrived on a chartered launch from Bluff after dark. They had to stay the night as their launch's rotor suddenly disappeared – no charges laid!

Flying in DC3s throughout the country when you had to walk up a gradient to your seat; the unreal experience at the time of flying with propellers spinning silently on the first turbo-prop aircraft to be introduced into domestic service in New Zealand, in an NAC Viscount between Christchurch and Auckland the week they were introduced in 1958.

Acknowledgements

I am grateful for the support and enthusiasm I have received from so many people as I researched, photographed and wrote this book. I first thank two friends, Peter and Margaret Findlay, who kindly drove us over many roads in the Nelson district to obtain many photographs and facts. The person who first suggested I should create this book was Peter Bush, a colleague from my days on the *New Zealand Herald* and the *Weekly News* in the 1950s who went on to become well known in the world of rugby photography. There were times I wondered whether it was such a good idea, lugging cameras and laptop computers on and off planes, long days at the wheel of a motorcar, negotiating ice and snow or coping with the heat of summer.

My wife, Anne, travelled with me and was always on hand for support when the going got tough, when the weather turned nasty and we decided to relax with a glass of wine and wait for the skies to clear. I received assistance from many people throughout the land and I apologise if someone has not been acknowledged.

I first thank postcard collectors for the use of cards from their collections: Yvonne Coles and Brian McClintock of Auckland, John and Merle Sneddon of Levin, Simon Crawford, William Main and Alistair Robb of Wellington and Laurence Eagle of Christchurch. The late James Taylor of Christchurch who gave valuable advice.

To John Sullivan, Joan McCracken and Betty Moss of the Alexander Turnbull Library; Archives New Zealand; Mary Lewis of the Hocken Library, Dunedin; Wendy and David Rhodes of *New Zealand Memories* magazine; Wayne Harman, associate editor, *New Zealand Herald*; Lauri Tapsell, manager, editorial resources, *New Zealand Herald*; Audrey Burtscher of Tekapo, who kindly hunted out historic photographs of the district; Alan and Brigie Pollock for Queenstown research; Bill Prebble for Denniston Mine assistance; and Barry O'Donnell for the maps, thank you all for your enthusiasm to assist.

To the professional photographers who kindly undertook assignments for this book: Murray Lloyd and Fiona Morris of Wellington, www.murraylloyd.com; Donald Lamont of Alexandra, http://donaldlamont.blogspot.com; and Simon Darby, Alpine Image, Wanaka, www.alpineimages.co.nz, thank you for the great images!

From north to south I thank with sincerity: Lynda Hamond, Far North Regional Museum of Kaitaia; Louise Fincham, Intercity Group (NZ), Fullers Bay of Islands; Claire Nodder, collections manager, Whangarei Museum and Heritage Park; Heather Ayrton, Rawene; Robin Hoare of Rawene for photographs old and new; Michael Lawton, Kauri Museum, Matakohe; Darcy and Trish Sterling of Matakohe; Peter Marsh, Albertland Museum; Patsy Montgomery, manager, Waipu Museum; A.S. Harris; Jonathan Knox and Nicky Brookes of Qualmark New Zealand; Bill Cousins, Auckland; Bill Francis, Waiheke Island; Kelvin Hynes, Coromandel; Frances Burton, Thames; Trev Terry, Hamilton; Kevin Ward, Hamilton; Joan Stanley, Matamata Historical Society; Bruce and Cilla White; Darryl Gallagher and Jane Strachan, Rotorua Museum of Art and History; Paula Karkkainen, Whakatane Museum and Gallery; Ann Paynter, Opotiki Museum; D.C. Sheppard; Geni Johnston, Taupo Museum; Alan Webb, Regent Theatre, Te Awamutu; Gray Clapman, Gisborne, whose book *Blue Sky Highway* is a treasure; Rosheen Parker, Central Hawke's Bay Settler's Museum; Kerri Garaway and Kathy Guy, Bayview Chateau Tongariro; David McDermid, manager, and John Gray, Whanganui Riverboat Centre; Eketahuna and Districts Early Settlers Museum; Gareth Winter and Jenny Davidson, Wairarapa Archive collection; Paul Williams and Mark Round, *Dominion Post*; Colin McDiarmid, Wellington, for the panoramas of Wellington rugby grounds Athletic Park and the new Westpac Stadium; my old friend Michael Box, Wellington, for proof reading; Tom Brow, Wellington, best view in town;   Denis Clode, Wellington, for colour advice; Mark Cole, New Zealand Railway and Locomotive Society; Noel Meek; Graeme Jupp, Wellington; Mary Mountier and Garry Ward, Waikanae Beach, for their kind assistance; Bob Stott, Wellington; Richard Westlake, Wellington, special thanks; Simon Woolf, Wellington, the Yousuf Karsh of New Zealand photography; Chris Brown, Edwin Fox Society, Picton; Nelson Provincial Museum; Tasman Bay Heritage Trust; David Panckhurst for Reefton references; Jane Wells, Blackball Hotel; History House, Greymouth; Ron Alexander, Rangiora; Tim Jones, librarian, Christchurch Art Gallery; David Hinman, Christchurch; Bill Angus of the Estate of Rita Angus; D.L.A. Turner, Christchurch, colour of the Otago Rail Trail and Kingston; Graham Radcliffe, Christchurch; Roy Sinclair, Christchurch; Jennifer Murray, Tekapo; Denis Callesen, manager, The Hermitage, Mount Cook; Brent Fafeita, Sir Edmund Hillary Alpine Centre and Museum; Rowan Carroll, director, North Otago Museum; Ian Dougherty, Dunedin; Stew Robertson, Advertising and Art, Dunedin; Olsen and Hardwicke Knight, Otago Cavalcade; Rowan Carroll, director, and Kathleen Stringer, curator, North Otago Museum; Jill Haley, archivist, Otago Settlers Museum; Barbara Reid, Taeri Gorge Railway; Bill Cowan, Dunedin; Matt Rhodes, Skippers Canyon Jet, Queenstown; Peter and Vicki Byrne, Cardrona Hotel; Doug South; Nicky Brookes, Real Journeys; old friend Reginald McGovern, Redwood City, California, USA; and John Winlove, for organising a four-wheel drive safari into the rugged heartland of the South Island.

To Lorraine Olphert, friend and editor of Grantham House manuscripts for many years, for her dedication to the English language; and our printers, Peter Ho, Shirley Mo-Ku and Chu Kam Siu, for their attention to detail and quality which has been their hallmark for the past 25 years.

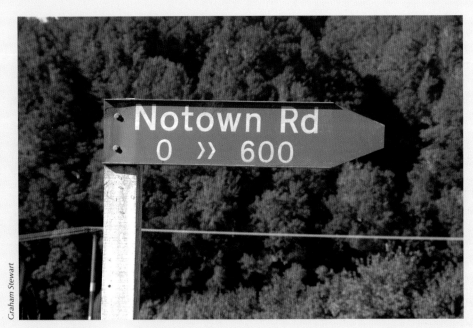

Graham Stewart

The road to the Notown Cemetery on the West Coast of the South Island.

Index

Page numbers in italics refer to an illustration.

A

advertising *108, 113, 194, 227, 260, 296, 306*
Akaroa *249*
Alexandra *290*
All Blacks *16*, 91, *186, 187*
Americans 313
Angus, Rita *251*
Anscombe, Edmund and Associates 155
Antarctica 266
Anzac Day *201*
Aoraki Mount Cook Percival Village 258
apples 196
Arapuni 111
Aratiatia Rapids 111
Arbour Day 166
Armed Constabulary 108, 145
Arrowtown *295*
Art Deco 147
Art Union man 59
Arthur's Pass 221, *250*
Ashburton *252*
Auckland *49-67*
  Auckland Bus Company 59
  Auckland Public Library and Art Gallery *65*
  Bayswater 56
  Birkenhead 5
  Devonport *52, 53*, 56
  Ellerslie races 61
  Farmers Trading Company *62*
  Hobson Street *62*
  Khyber Pass Road 66
  Kohimaramara 49
  Lumsden Green, Newmarket 66
  Mission Bay 51
  MOTAT *253*
  Newmarket 58, 66
  Paritai Drive *51*
  Ponsonby *50*, 58, 63
  Queen Street *58-60, 63-65*
  Remuera 48

  Sky Tower *62, 64*
  Stanley Bay 56
  Tamaki Drive *49, 51*
  Victoria Street East *12*
  Victoria Street West *64*
  Waitemata Harbour *52-57*
  Wellesley Street East *65*
  Westhaven *55*
Aupouri Peninsula 20
Automobile Association 15
aviation *88, 194, 253, 320*

B

baby buggies *234*
backpackers 43, 95
Balclutha *282*
Baldwin steam tram *126*
band rotundas *136, 137, 194, 195, 315*
Bank of New South Wales *26, 262, 263*
Bank of New Zealand *22, 63, 70, 121, 162, 208, 268, 315*
Bank of Otago *262, 263*
Banks, Joseph 104, 248
Banks Peninsula 249
Batten, Jean *88*
Battle of Gate Pa 73, 90
Bay of Islands *26-33*
Bay of Islands Vintage Railway *35*
Bay of Plenty *85, 90-93*
Bayne, Pete 318
Beca Carter Hollings and Ferner 222
birds 21, 87, 142, 228, 319
Bishops
  Marsden 25
  Selwyn 19
Blackball *213*
Blackball Shipping Line 213
Blackwell, George 232
Blake, Sir Peter *56*

326

Bledisloe, Lord and Lady 26
Blenheim *194,195*
  Cleghorn Memorial Band Rotunda *194, 195*
Bluff *2, 316*
Booth, Sir Alfred 165
Bowen Falls 306
boysenberries 196
Bridges
  Alexandra *290*
  Auckland *54-56*
  Balclutha *282*
  Christchurch, Colombo Street *244*
  Christchurch, Hamish Hay *242-243*
  Christchurch, Victoria Street *242*
  Gisborne, Peel Street *107*
  Greymouth *218*
  Hamilton *74*
  Kaiapoi *232*
  Lower Hutt *172*
  Manuherikia viaduct *287*
  Mataura *311*
  New Plymouth, Poet's *136, 137*
  oldest stone-arched 36
  Orewa *47*
  Otira viaduct *222, 223*
  Poolburn viaduct *286, 287*
  Taramakau *220*
  Tauranga 92
  upper-truss wooden *1*
  Wairoa *143*
  Wanganui, Dublin Street *128*
  Whakarewarewa *87*
  Wingatui viaduct *280*
Brightwater 202
British colonial forces 90
Britomart Station *60*
Brunner, Sir Thomas 216
Buildings
  Auckland, City Chambers *64*
  Auckland, Customhouse *61*
  Auckland, Endeans 59
  Auckland, Ferry *57*
  Auckland, New Zealand Loan and Mercantile
    61
  Auckland, Palmerston *59*
  Auckland, West Plaza *61*
  Auckland, Wingates *59*
  Christchurch, Canterbury University College
    241

Christchurch, Fisher *238*
Christchurch, J Ballantyne and Company *239*
Christchurch, Royal Exchange *236*
Christchurch, Telecom *236*
Dunedin, Larnach Castle *267*
Dunedin, Law Courts *267*
Dunedin, Stock Exchange *268*
Hastings, Municipal *156*
Hastings, Westermans *155*
Hokitika, Carnegie Free Library *224*
Napier, Public Trust *151*
Oamaru, Forrester Gallery *262*
Te Aroha, Cadman bathhouse 78
Buses
  Chateau Tongariro *112*
  Clyde, charabanc *291*
  Oamaru, Searle's motorbus *15*
  Rotorua *85*
  Wanganui *126*
  Wilmot Pass *310*
Buck, Sir Peter *158*
Bull, James 126
Buller Gorge *210, 211*
Bulls *126*
bungy-jumping 110, 299
Burns, Rev. Thomas 267
Busby, James 26, 28
Butler, Rev. John Gare 25
butter 132, 201
buzzy bees 82

C

Cambridge *75*, 111
  Caravan Club *15*
  GPO Bar and Brasserie *75*
Cambridge, Duke of 75
Campbell, Sir John Logan *64*
canoe, Mataatua *94*
canoe routes 83, 129
Canterbury Association 233, 248, 252
Canterbury Pilgrims 233, 248
Canterbury Plains 221, 223, 259
Canterbury, South *249-261*
Cape Brett *32*
Cape Reinga *20, 21*
  lighthouse *20*
caravans *15*
Cardrona *294*

Cargill, Captain William 267, 313
Carnegie, Andrew 224
carrot capital 117
Carter, Charles Rooking 165
Carterton *165*
    daffodil capital 165
Cass *251*
Catlins 282
caves 81
centennial celebrations 1940 27, 170
Central Otago *285-294*
champagne 242
Chapman-Taylor, James 157
Charleston *214*
Chateau Tongariro *112, 113*
cheese 132, 201
Chinese 205
Chong, Chew 132
Christchurch 223, *233-247*
    ANZ Bank *237*
    Diamond Jubilee Clock Tower *240*
    New Brighton Pier *246, 247*
Churches
    Christchurch Cathedral *235*
    Dunedin, Knox Presbyterian *27*
    Dunedin, St Joseph's Catholic Cathedral *272*
    East Coast, Raukokore Anglican *97*
    Invercargill, St Andrew's Presbyterian *315*
    Kerikeri, St James *25*
    Lake Tekapo, Church of Good Shepherd *254*
    Lower Hutt, St James Anglican *172*
    Matakohe, Coates Memorial *41*
    Nelson Cathedral *197*
    Ohinemutu, St Faith's Anglican *84*
    Palmerston North, All Saints Anglican *125*
    Russell, Christ Church *31*
    Tauranga, St George's *90*
    Tikitiki, St Mary's Anglican *100*
Clark, Rt Hon. Helen 66
Clark, Russell 38
Claudlands 74
Cleghorn, Dr George 195
Clinton *284*
Clyde *291*
Clyde Dam 280, 287, 292
coal 201, *206, 207*, 208, 212, 213, 216, 221, 283
coastal shipping 48, *98, 102*, 127, 179
Coates, Rt Hon. Joseph Gordon *41*
Coates, Tom 40

Cobham, Lord 54
Colenso, William 147
Collingwood *201*
Collingwood, Admiral Lord 201
Collins, Tudor *39, 41*
container port *176*
Cook, James 21, 23, 71, 98, 102, *104*, 122, 147, 190, 248, 267, 309
Cornwall, Duke and Duchess 85
Coromandel Peninsula 56, *71, 80*
Coronet Peak 299
cows 18
Craig Craig and Moller, architects 64
crayfish 230
Cromwell *292*
Crowther and McAuley 145
cyclists *217*, 242, 243, *287*

D

dairy factories 77, 132, 134
Danish migrants 160
Dannevirke *160*
Danseys Pass Coach Inn *2*
Dargaville *40*
Dargaville, Joseph 40
Darwin, Charles 19, 31
Dean, Minnie 312
Deans, William and John 233
Deeming, J.C. 29
Deep Cove 308
Denniston *206, 207*
Department of Conservation 39, 207, 287
Desert Road *114*
De Surville, St Jean Marie 21
'Devil's Boots', Rockville *200*
Devil's Staircase *301*
Dictionary of the New Zealand Language 28
disasters *118, 148-151, 174, 175, 239*
Dobson, Sir Arthur 223, 250
dogs 37, 204, *318*
Dolomite Point 215
dolphin, Opo 38
Domett, Alfred 146
Doubtful Sound *308, 309*
Doubtless Bay 23
Duke of York (King George V1) 203
Duncan, George Smith 272
Dunedin *267-279*

Baldwin Street, *278, 279*
Barker family 267
Dunedin Technical School *276*
High Street *270, 271*
King Edward High School *276*
Mornington *269*
Otago Polytechnic *276*
Rattray Street *272, 273*
Threave House *269*
Dunedin and Port Chalmers Railway Company 275
Dunstan *291*
d'Urville Island 190

E

earthquakes 123, 128, 130, 143, *146-151*, 153, 154, 162, 164, 165, *204*
Eastbourne Borough Council 67
Eastland (East Coast) *95-103*
Eden, Sir Anthony 33
Edinburgh, Duke of *43*
Edmonds Cookery Book 244
Edmonds, Thomas John 244
Edward VII, King 132, 224
Egmont Community Arts Council 133
Egmont National Park 131
Eketahuna *162*
electric light *212*
Eltham *132*
Emigrants and Colonists Aid Corporation Limited 123
energy production 131, 134
European settlers 171, 312

F

Fairlie 256, *259*
Fairlight 302
Farming
dairy *18,* 19, 77
sheep *2-5,* 68
Featherston *166*
Feilding *123*
Feilding, Lieutenant-Colonel William, 123
Ferries
Auckland *56, 57*
Albatross 52
Kestrel 52, 91
Makora 57

Muritai 67
Ngoiro 56, 57
Pupuke 57
Takapuna 57
The Peregrine 57
Ferries car
Auckland
Goshawk 52
Kohukohu-Rawene *36, 37*
Kohu Ra Tuarau 37
Opua 29
Doris 29
Okiato 29
Queenstown
Antrim 295
Earnslaw 295, 298, 299, 302
Mountaineer 298
Ben Lomond 298
river pontoons 1
Stewart Island *320*
Ulva 320
Awarua 320
James O'Brien 320
Matai 320
Southland 320
Theresa Ward 320
Wairua 320
Wairua (new) 320
Wellington-Lyttelton *192, 193, 248*
Arahanga 193
Arahura 192
Aramoana 193
Aranui 193
Aratere 193
Aratika 193
Condor Vitesse 193
Incat (046) 193
Kaitaki 192
Lynx (Incat 057) 193
Maori 248, 249
Monte Stello 192
Santa Regina 192
Tamahine 193
The Condor 10 193
Wahine 175, 179
Fiordland *305-310*
Fiordland National Park *309*
Fire brigades 107

Fires 30, 36, 38, 64, 72, 76, 79, 95, 130, 138, *148 -151*, 154, 162, 201, *239*, 257, 303, 307, 313
First World War 166
fish and chips 23
fishing 98, 310
Fitzsimmons, Bob 260
flax 201, 316
Flett, John 80
floods 297
Forgotten World Highway *138-140*
Forty-fifth parallel of latitude 298
Forty Mile Bush 161, 162
four-wheel-drive vehicles *14*
Foveaux Strait 316
Fox Glacier *226*
Fox, Sir William 227
Franz Josef Glacier *226*
French 147, 249
Freyberg, Sir Bernard *185*
frozen meat 263, 266
fruit-growing 155, 199, 292

G

Garnett, Albert 156
George V, King 225
Georgetown 315
German settlers 196
geysers 86, 88
Gisborne *104-107*
    Robinson Memorial Clock tower 105
Gisborne, William 107
glaciers *226, 227*, 256
Glen Murray *11*
Glendowie 51
Glenhope 202, *203*
Godley, John Robert 233
godwits 21
gold 80, 201, 205, 208, 212, 214, 216, 220, 223- *225*, 289, 291, 292, 294-296, 300
Golden Bay *199*
Gore 284, 302, *311*
Gore-Brown, Sir Thomas 194
Gore, country and western 311
government 44
Government Tourist Corporation 109, 142, 227, 294, 303
Governors and Governors-General *26, 50, 54, 65*, 166, *184*, 187, 194, 216, 255

Graham, Robert 46
grape vines 2, 3, 4
greenstone 220, 223, 228
Grey, Sir George 166, 216
Grey, Zane 33
Greymouth *216-219*
Greytown *166*
Griffin, A.R. 224
Grono, Captain John 306
Grunman Widgeon seaplanes *303, 320*
gumboots 82, 119

H

Haast *228*, 293
Halfmoon Bay *318*
Hall, Dinah 31
Halley's Comet 66
Hamilton *73*
Hamilton Borough Council 74
Hamilton, Captain John, RN 73
Hanmer Springs 229
Hannah, Robert 214
Hanson, Dr Fridtjof 133
Hapuawhenua viaduct 121
Hardie Boys, Sir Michael 187
Harper, Leonard 226
Hastings *154-156*
Hauraki Plains 80
Hawera *130*
Hawke's Bay *143-159*
Hawks Crag *210, 211*
Havelock 190
Havelock North *10, 157*
Hay, Peter Seton 121
Hay, Sir Hamish Grenfell 242
Heaphy Track *201, 205*
Helensville *48*
Heretaunga Plains 154
Heriot 282
Hermitage *256-258*
Hicks Bay *98*
Hillary, Sir Edmund *258*
Historic Places Trust 11, 25
Hitler, Adolf 261
Hokianga Harbour *36-38*
Hokitika *224*
Hokonui moonshine whisky 311
Holland, Rt Hon. Sidney 152

Hollyford Valley 304
horses
  horse-drawn cabs *12, 216, 234, 314*
  horse-drawn carriages *13*
  horse-drawn trams *58, 63, 196, 198,* 220, *233,*
    235, 268, 270, 275, 313
  horse-drawn vehicles *23, 40, 41, 103, 144, 164,*
    198, 200, 221, 250, 256
  horse-racing 61
  horse trough *12*
  six-horse team *11*
  thoroughbred horse studs 75
hot soda water geyser 78
hot springs *46, 48, 78, 84, 89,* 109, *229*
Hotels
  Adelphi, Kaikoura *230*
  Albert, Hastings *154*
  Arcadia, Levin *170*
  Auckland *61*
  Blackball *213*
  Brian Boru, Thames 69
  Cardrona *294*
  Central, Auckland *12*
  Charleston *214*
  City, Charleston *214*
  City, Wellington *184*
  Clarendon, Napier *147*
  Club at Bluff *316*
  Club, Eketahuna *162*
  Club, Opunake *133*
  Colonial, Puhoi *46*
  Commercial, Te Awamutu *77*
  Commercial, Whangarei *43*
  Coronation, Eltham *132*
  Criterion, Napier *147*
  Dawson's, Reefton *212*
  Duke of Marlborough, Russell *30*
  Dunstan, Clyde *291*
  Eichardt's, Queenstown *296, 297*
  Empire, Ross *225*
  Empire, Wellington *182*
  European, Charleston *214*
  Fox Glacier *227*
  Gleesons *62*
  Grand, Palmerston North *125*
  Grand, Whangarei *43*
  Hampden, Murchison *204*
  Harbour View, Raglan *76*
  Homer tunnel *304,* 305

Houhora Tavern *22*
Hukatere, 22
Junction, Takaka *199*
Junction, Thames *69*
Karamea *205*
Lake House, Waikaremoana *142*
Langholm, Mangaweka *121*
Manutahi, Ruatoria *100*
Masonic, Dannevirke *160*
Masonic, Napier *146, 150*
Masonic, Opotiki 95
Masonic, Tauranga 85
Milford Sound *306, 307*
Miller's Commercial Inn and Tavern, Wellington
  182
New Commercial, Eketahuna *162*
Northern Wairoa, Dargaville *40*
Nottingham Castle, Morrinsville *79*
Opononi *38*
Oxford on Avon, Christchurch *244*
Oxleys, Picton *191*
Pukekohe *68*
Revingtons, Greymouth 217
Rob Roy, Waihi *80*
Royal Albert, Dunedin *275*
Royal, Featherston *166*
Royal George, Auckland *66*
Royal, Opotiki 95
Ship, Nelson *198*
Southern Cross, Dunedin *270, 271*
Southland Tavern *315*
South Sea, Stewart Island *318*
Star and Garter, Coromandel *71*
Tarawera Tavern *144*
Te Anau *303*
Te Kaha *96*
Te Puke *94*
Terminus, Otira *221*
Terraces, Taupo *109*
The Wharf, The Park, The Lady Bowen, Thames
  70
Tramway, Taramakau *220*
United Service, Christchurch *237*
Vulcan, St Bathans *289*
Waipu, Ngaruawahia *73*
Wairakei *109*
Waitemata *61*
Waitomo Caves *81*
Waiwera Hot Springs *46*

Wanaka *294*
  Whangamomona *138, 139*
  White Hart, Hawera *130*
  Winton *312*
Houhora *22*
Howard, Mabel 237
Howell, Captain John 312
Huka Falls 110, 111
Hukarere Maori Girls' College 152
Hundertwasser, Friedensreich 35
Hunter, George 122
Hunterville *122*
Hunterville, Taylors general store 121
Huntley 122
Huntly 111
Hutchins, Les and Olive 309
hydro-electric power stations, 111, 212, 291, 310,
  316

I

International Date Line 105
Invercargill *313-315*
  Georgetown 315
  Gladstone 313
  Troopers' Memorial *315*
  Waikiwi 313

J

jaffa race 279
James, Billy T 132
Japan 311
Japanese prisoner-of-war camp 166
jet-boating 110, 299
Jones, Bryn M. 258
J. Wattie Canneries Limited *154*

K

Kahurangi National Park 201, 205
Kaiapoi *232*
Kaikohe *34*
Kaikoura *230*
Kaipara 41, 48
Kaitaia *22*
Kaitangata *282*
Kaitangata Railway and Coal Company 282
Kaiti Beach 104
Karamea 201 *205*

Karapiro 111
Kawakawa *35*
Kawakawa Bay 99
kauri 23, *39*, 40
kauri gum 22, 40
Kauri Museum *41*
Kemp, Charlotte 25
Kemp House *25*
Kemp, James 25
Kerikeri *25*
Kerikeri Mission House *25*
Kenepuru Sound 190
'Kestrel at the Landing' *91*
King Country *81-83*
King, Dr Truby 188
Kingston 299, 301, *302*
Kingston Flyer *302*, 311, 312
kiwi 87, 142, 228, 319
kiwifruit 90, 94, 196
Kohukohu *36*
Kororareka *30*
Kumara 220, 224
Kupe 23

L

Lake Manapouri underground power station 310,
  316
Lake Wakatipu Shipping Company 295
Lakes
  Blue, St Bathans 289
  Dunstan *292*
  Manapouri *309*
  Rotoiti 211
  Rotorua *84*
  Taupo *108*
  Te Anau *306*
  Tekapo *254, 255*
  Waikaremoana *142*
  Wakatipu *295, 298, 299, 301*
  Wanaka *294*
Land Wars 134, 147
Larnach Castle *267*
Larnach, William 267
Launches
  Alma G., Bay of Islands *32*
  Constance, Doubtful Sound 308, 309
  Doris, Opua *29*
  Fullers catamaran, Bay of Islands *32*

332

Kewpie Too, Bay of Islands *32*
  Ruapani, Lake Waikaremoana 142
Lawson, Robert 262
'Lemon and Paeroa' *80*
Letheridge, Hannah King 31
Levin *170*
Levin, W.H. 170
limestone *200, 215, 241, 262*
liquor polls 80
longest place name in the world *159*
Lord of the Rings, 79
Lovelock, John Edward (Jack) *261*
Lower Hutt *172, 173*
Lumsden 302
Lumsden Green, Newmarket *66*
Lyell 204
Lyttelton 233, *248*

M

Mace, Fred 81
Mair, Gilbert 31
Makohine viaduct *121*
Manapouri-Doubtful Sound Tourist Company 308, 309
Manawatu *119*
Manawatu Gorge *14*
Manchester Block 123
Mangaonoho *120*
Mangatainoka 161
Mangaweka *121*
Mangaweka viaduct 121
Mangonui *23*
Maniototo *287, 288*
Mansfield, Katherine *188*
Maori 31, 49, 51, 73, 77, 81, 82, 84, 86, 87, 94,
  104, 108, 124, 134, 147, 155, 171, 194, 196,
  201, 205, 208, 216, 223, 230, 233, 248, 264,
  282, 294, 306, 311, 312, 319
carver 100
culture centre 87
Chiefs, 28
  'George' Te Ara 24
  Tane Tinorau 81
  Te Ati Awa 173
  Te Kooti 83, 108
  Te Rauparaha 170
  Tukawaiki 317
haka *16, 27*

Kings
  Tawhiao 73, 82, 83
  Tuheitia Paki 73
Leader
  Princess Te Puea *73*
Tribes
  Arawa 88
  Muaupoko 170
  Ngai Tahu 267
  Ngapuhi 49
  Ngati Porou 100
  Ngati Tara 171
  Ngati Toa 170, 311
  Ngati Tuwharetoa 108, 113
  Ngati Whatua 49, 51
  Ngatikahu 23
  Tainui 49
  Te Arawa 100
  Te Ati Awa 191
  Te Atiawe 134
  Te Ngati Kahungunu 147
  Te Puoho 311
  Tuhoe 142
  Tuhourangi Ngati Wahiao 86
  Whatonga 171
Kapu te rangi pa 94
Orakei Pa 51
Te Whare Runanga meeting house *27*
Tiwakawaka 94
Toi people 94
Toroa 94
Turangawaewae marae 73
villages 83, 86, 87
Whanau-a-Apanui people 96

market gardens 68
Marlborough *191-195*
Marlborough Sounds 191
marlin 24, 32, 33
Marmite 82
Marsden Point 42
Marsh, Dame Ngaio *237*
Martha Mine 80
Martin, John 167
Martinborough *167*
Marton 120, *122*
Masters, Joseph 163
Masterton *163, 164*
  Golden Shears 163

Matakohe *41*, 45
  Tudor Collins Wing 39
Matamata *79*
Matatote viaduct 121
Matauri *311*
Maunganui o te Ao viaduct 121
McCahon, Colin 260
McCombes, Elizabeth *237*
McConnell Smith Limited 222
McKenzie Country *255*, 259
McKenzie, James 255
McKenzie, Roderick 225
McLean, Gavin, 98
McLeod, Rev. Norman 44
medical, first operations 195
Mercer *72*, 111
Mercer, Captain (Air Travel NZ) 306
merchant warehouses *178*
Milford Sound *304-307*
military settlements 73, 75, 166
miners *80*
Mission Stations, *19*, 25, 28, 147
Mission vineyards 147
missionaries 94
Moeraki Boulders *264, 265*
Mohaka viaduct *143*
Mokena 78
Moki tunnel *140*
Mokoia Island *84*
Morrinsville *79*
Morris, Di 318
Motorcars, *14*, *15*, *34*, *66*, *81*, *133*, *141*, *168*,
  238, 312
  Austin Seven *47*
  De Dions *256*
  Ford Consul *66*
  Model T Ford *17*
  Vauxhall Velox *66*
Motu Wai (Red Island) 24
Motueka *199*
Motukokako Island *32*
Mount Aspiring National Park *228*, 293
Mount Cook Motor Company *256*
Mount Drury Reserve *92*
Mount Mauao Reserve *92*
Mount Maunganui 92, 93
Mountains
  Cook 258

Hobson 49
Kaikouri Range 230
Marble 199
Maungakiekie (One Tree Hill) 49, 64
Maungawhau (Mt Eden) 49
Mitre Peak 305-307
Murchison 204
Ngauruhoe 113
Puketoi 161
Remarkables 296
Rochfort 206
Ruahine Range 161
Ruapehu 111, 113, 118, 157
Taranaki/Egmont 2, 131, 136, 137, 141
Tararua Range 161
Te Aroha 78
Tongariro 113, 129
Victoria 52
Waepapa 161
Wellington 49
Mountbatten, Earl and Countess 32
Murchison 204, 209
museums 41, 170, 171, 224, 241, 253
mussels 190

N

Napier 146-153
  Ahuriri 153
  Girls' High School 153
  'Pania of the Reef' 152
  Napier Thirty Thousand Club 152
National Bank of New Zealand 64, 130, 262
native birds 142, 228
native trees 142
natural gas 131
Navy 150
Nelson 196-198, 311
  first city 196
New Plymouth 134-137
  Pukekura Park 136, 137
New Zealand Company 127, 171, 173, 196, 233,
  267
New Zealand Government Railways 295
New Zealand Labour Party 213
Nga Tawa 122
New Zealander's firsts
  first to climb Mount Everest *258*
  first to fly UK to NZ *88*

first to split the atom 190, *202*
first votes for women *237*
first woman mayor (British Empire) 65
Ngaruawahia *73*, 111
Ngata, Sir Apirana *27*, 99, 100, *158*
Ninety Mile Beach 22
'Nippon clip-ons' 54
Norsewood 160
North British freezing works, Napier *153*
North Canterbury *229-232*
North Island *17-188*
North Island Main Trunk *72*, 82, 83, *116*, 117, *118*, 119, *120*, *121*, 122
Northcote *54*, 56
Norwegian migrants 160

O

Oamaru *15, 262, 263*
  Forrester Gallery *262*
Ohaeawai *34*
Ohakune *117*
Ohinemutu *84*
Ohingaiti 121
oil fields 131
Opo (dolphin) 38
Opononi *38*
  Andrews, A.S. and Sons *38*
Opotiki *95*
Opua *29*
Opunake *133*
Orakau, battle of 83
orchards 196
Orewa *47*
Otago *280-284*
Otago Central Rail Trail *286, 287*
Otago coastline 265
Otaki 170
Otehei Bay *33*
Otira *221*
Otira viaduct *222, 223*
Otorohanga *82*
oysters 316

P

Pacific Ocean *20, 21*, 230, 231
Paekakariki *170*
'Paekok Pie' 170
Pahiatua *161*

Paihia *28*
Palmerston, Lord 124
Palmerston North 120, *124, 125*
Paparoa National Park 215
Parakai hot mineral springs 48
Parititahi tunnels *231*
Parliament Buildings *183*
parliamentary tour, Northland *14*
Pascoe, John 215
Pattrick, Jenny 207
pavlova 82
Pearce, Richard William *253*
Pelorus Sound 190
penguins 97
perambulators *13, 234, 245*
Petone 173
Phar Lap 260
Pickering, Sir William 190
Picton *191-193*
Pierre, Bill 116
Plimmer, John 182, *182*
ploughing *11*
Plunket Society 188
Plymouth Company ships 134
pohutukawa 21, *99*
Polish refugees 161
Pomare, Sir Maui *158*
Pompallier House *19*
Porangahau 159
Porritt, Sir Arthur 255
Port Albert *15*
Port Chalmers *266*
Portland 42
Post Offices
  Auckland *59, 60*
  Bluff *316*, 320
  Cambridge *75*
  Carterton *165*
  Christchurch *236*
  Dargaville *40*
  Feilding *123*
  Gisborne 105
  Gore *311*
  Greymouth *216*
  Highgate, Dunedin *276*
  Invercargill *315*
  Mangonui *23*
  Martinborough *167*
  Masterton *164*

New Plymouth *135*
Ohaeawai *34*
Palmerston North *124*
Rangiora *232*
Taihape *119*
Tokomaru Bay *101*
Wakefield *202*
Wanganui *128*
Westport *209*
postage stamp *68*
postcards 136
Poverty Bay *104-107*
Presidential Highway *284*
Prime Ministers and Premiers *41, 66,* 138, 209, 222, 224, *252,* 316
Prince of Wales (Edward VII) 203
Public Works Department 51, 121
Puhoi *46*
Pukekohe *68*
Punakaiki pancake rocks *215*

Q

Queen Charlotte Sound 191
Queen Elizabeth II *43, 68*
Queen Elizabeth Square *59*
Queenstown and Lakes District *295-303*
Queenstown *2, 295-299*
Queen Victoria 72, 196, 240, 275, 296

R

Raglan *76*
Raglan, Lord 76
Railcar Rm32 *143*
Railcar Rm53 *286*
railways 29, *35, 43,* 48, *58, 60, 68, 72-74, 77, 81, 82, 83, 90, 115, 116, 118, 120, 121,*122, *124, 125, 143, 155, 160, 161, 163, 166, 169, 170, 177,* 179, *202, 203, 206, 207, 218-221, 250, 251,* 252, 256, 259, 267, *280, 281, 283, 284, 286-288, 302,* 311, 312, *315*

Railway Stations
Arthur's Pass *250*
Auckland *60*
Clinton *284*
Dunedin *275*
Glenhope *203*
Greymouth *219*
Mercer *72*

Paekakariki *170*
Raurimu *116*
Waiouru *115*
Rakiura National Park 319
Rangiora *232*
Rangiriri 111
Rangitaiki *145*
Rangitikei *119-122*
Raramal tunnels *231*
raspberries 196
Rawene *37*
Raurimu *116*
Reefton *212*
Rees, William 296
Reeves, Sir Paul *184*
Richardson and Company 98
Rimutaka Incline *169*
Rimutaka Range *166, 168*

Rivers
Aorere *201*
Aparima *312*
Ashburton 252
Ashley 232
Avon 233, *242-244*
Buller *210, 211*
Clutha *282, 283, 290, 291, 292*
Grey 213, 216, 217, *218, 219*
Hatea 42
Inangahua 212
Kaiapoi 232
Kawarau *292*
Lyvia 308
Mahurangi 45
Makarewa 313
Manawatu *1*
Mangatainoka 161
Mataura *311*
Ngaruroro 147
Northern Wairoa 40
Ohinemuri 80
Oreti 313
Oruaiti 23
Taipa 23
Taramakau *220, 223*
Turanganui 104
Waikato *72, 73, 74, 111*
Waimakariri *223, 232*
Waipa 73, 82, 111
Waipoua *163*

336

Whakatane 94
Whangaehu *118*
Whanganui 83, *127-129*
Riverton *312*
Roads
   Auckland to Whangarei 42
   Desert Road *114*
   Devil's Elbow 301
   Devil's Staircase *301*
   Eltham *132*
   Forgotten World Highway *140*
   Helensville to Port Albert *15*
   Homer tunnel *304*
   Lewis Pass 212
   Lyttelton road tunnel 248
   Main Waitohi Road 253
   Mangaweka to Hunterville 122
   Maungaturoto *40*
   Napier to Taupo *144, 145*
   Parititahi and Raramai tunnels *231*
   Rimutaka hill *168*
   Skippers Canyon *300*
   Skippers Canyon Jet *300*
   Taihape *119*
   Taranaki *141*
Robin, May 152
Robison, Hugh 263
Ross *225*
Rotorua 74, *84-89*
   Bath House *89*
   Prince's Gate *85*
   Rotorua Museum of Art and History 89
   Te Puia *87*
   Tudor Towers *89*
   Whakarewarewa *86, 87*
Royal tours *43*, 64, *68*, 85
Ruatoria *100*
rugby *16, 91, 186, 187*
Russell *2, 19, 29-31*
Russell, Ivy *312*
Rutherford, Sir Ernest 190, *202*

S

St Bathans *289*
St Clair, Dunedin *277*
St Heliers *49*, 51
St Heliers and Northcote Land Company 63
sanatorium 229

Satyanand, Hon. Anand *50*
Scandinavian migrants 162
Scott, Captain Robert Falcon 266
Scott, Sir George Gilbert 235
Scottish river names 313
Scottish settlers 311
Second World War 67, 215, 304
Seddon, Rt Hon. Richard 138, 209, 224
Semple, Hon. Robert 311
service station 110
Settlers Steamship Company 46
Shakespeare 132
sheep *2-5*, 83, 122, 293, 294, 296
sheepdog monument *255*
Sheppard, Kate *237*
Ship Cove 190
shipbuilding 42
Shipley, Rt Hon. Jenny 222, *252*
Ships
   Acheron 306
   Anna Watson 53
   Aurora 171
   Ballarat 160
   Boyd 24
   Charlotte Jane 233
   Commerce 24
   Comte de Paris 249
   Coromandel, HMS 71
   Cressy 233
   Diomede, HMS 150
   Dunedin 266
   Dunedin, HMS 150
   Edwin Fox 193
   Endeavour 21, 104
   Gothic 68
   Governor-Wynyard 53
   Hovding 160
   Jane 208
   John Wickliffe 267
   L'Aube 249
   Maersk Duffield 2
   Milburn Carrier II 248
   Pakura 98
   Pegasus 319
   Perseverance 316
   Philip Laing 267
   Queen Mary 2 53
   Queen Victoria 176
   Randolph 233

Ruapehu 176
Santa Regina 192
St Jean Baptiste 21
Sir George Seymour 233
Sonoma 91
Strathallan 260
Tamahine 193
Tasmanian Maid 208
Terra Nova '
Tory 171
Wahine 175, 179
Waimarie 129
Wairua 129
William Bryan 134
shopping 66, 69, 181
sightseeing cars 112
Sinclair, Roy 251
Sir Edmund Hillary Alpine Centre and Museum
    258
skiing 113, 117, 294, 299
Skippers Canyon 300
Small Arms Association 163, 165, 166
Snell, Peter 133
Somes Island 161
South African Boer War 315
South Island 189-317
South Port Island Harbour 316
Southern Alps 221, 226, 227
Southland 311-318
Southland Daily News 315
Southland Seafood Festival 316
Spectator, London 306
Spring Grove 202
State Highway One 72, 114, 121, 126, 231, 260,
    282, 317
steam locomotives 35, 51, 74, 302
steamships 45, 176, 178
Sterling, Mervyn 41
Sterling, Richard 41
Stewart, Anne 317
Stewart Dawson's, Wellington 182
Stewart Island 318-320
    Oban 318
Stewart Island Flights 320
Stirling, Duncan 97
Stirling Falls 306
Stirling Point 317
Stirling, William 317
Stone Store, Kerikeri 25

Stones, Anthony 104
Strait Shipping Company 192
Stratford 13, 132, 138
Stratford, glockenspiel clock tower 132
strawberries 196
strikes (industrial) 80, 213
Studholme, Michael 259
Suez Canal crisis 33
Sutherland, Donald 307
Sutherland Falls 307
Sutherland's Accommodation House 307
Sydney, Grahame 288

T
Taiapa, Pine 100
Taieri Gorge Railway 280, 281
Taihape 119, 121
Tairua Harbour 56
Takaka 199
Tane Mahuta 39
Tangiwai 118
Taonui viaduct 121
Taramakau 220
Taranaki 130-137
Taranaki Land Wars 134
Tasman, Abel 190, 199
Tasman Bay 196
Tasman Sea 20, 111, 129, 215
Taumarunui 83, 116, 120, 138
Taumata... 159
Taupo 108-111
    De Bretts Spa Resort 109
Tauranga 85, 90, 91
tax on dogs 37
Te Anau 303
Te Apiti wind farm 161
Te Araroa 99
Te Aroha 78
Te Aroha and District Museum 78
Te Aute College 158
Te Awamutu 77
Te Kaha 96
Te Kanawa, Dame Kiri 81
Te Kuiti 83
Te Mata Peak 157
Te Matua Ngahere 39
Te Poutapeta Bed and Breakfast 101
Te Puke 94

338

Te Rapa 120
Te Wahipounamu World Heritage area 309
Te Waimate Mission House *19*
Te Whare Runanga, Waitangi *27*
Te Urewera National Park *142*
telephone box *233*
Thames *69, 70*, 74
Theatres
  Auckland, Oxford *59*
  Auckland, Royal 64
  Christchurch, Regent *236*
  Hastings, Municipal *156*
  Invercargill, Majestic 315
  Stratford, TET Kings 132
thermal villages *84, 86, 87*, 88
Thomson, John 313
Three Mile Bush 165
Tikitiki *100*
Timaru *260, 261*
Timaru Boys' High School *261*
Timaru, Caroline Bay 260
timber 201, 216, 232, 259
Tiwai Point aluminium smelter 316
Tizard, Dame Catherine *65*
Todd, Charles *282*
Todd Corporation 282
Todd Energy 282
Todd Motors 282
Todd Petroleum 282
Tokomaru *101*
Tolaga Bay *102*
Tongariro National Park *113, 114*
tourism 88, 89, 207, 241, 264, 265, 294
town clocks *56, 75, 105, 119, 123, 124, 128, 135, 155, 164, 165, 194, 195, 209, 216, 224, 232, 236, 240, 247, 268, 311, 314, 316*
traction engine *10*
Trams
  battery *105-107*
  cable *171, 269, 271-273, 276*
  electric *49, 59, 61, 62, 65, 126-128, 134, 135, 147, 148, 153, 179, 234-238, 240-247, 267-269, 274, 276, 277, 313, 314-315*
  horse *58, 63, 196, 198, 220, 233, 235, 268, 270, 275, 313*
  steam *126, 247*
  wire *220*
Transit New Zealand 222
Transit of Mercury 1769 71

transport museums 45, 170, *253*
TranzAlpine Express *219, 250*
Treaty House *26*
trolley-buses *135, 245, 270*
Troup, George 267, 275
trout 108, 110, 142, 311
Tui Brewery 161
Turakina Maori Girls' College 122
Turangawaewae marae 73
Turoa Ski Fields 117
Tuturau 311

U
Ulstermen 94
Union Airways *194*
Union Steam Ship Company 193, 218
universities 267, 268
Upham, Captain Charles *230*
Upper Moutere 196
USA 311, 313
Utiku 121

V
VE and VJ Day celebrations 315
Victoria Conservation Park 212
Victorian postcards *86*
Von Haast, Julius 204, 226, 228

W
Waiheke Island *67*
Waihi *80*
Waikaremoana *142*
Waimate *259*
Waimate North *19*
Waiouru *115*
  Army Museum 115
Waiouru Snow Farm 294
Waipawa *158*
Waipoura Forest Sanctuary *39*
Waipu *44*
Waipu Bay 90
Waipukurau *158*
Wairakei *109*
Wairarapa *161-169*
Wairau Hospital 195
Wairau Plains 194
Waitangi *2, 16, 26, 27*

Waitohi Road 253
Waitomo Caves 81
Waiwera *46*
Waiwera hot springs 46
Wakamarina goldfields 190
Wakefield *202*
Wakefield, Arthur 202
Wakefield, Edward Gibbon 196, 233, 267
Walter Peak high-country farm 299
Wanaka *293, 294*
Wanganui *126-129*
Wanganui Collegiate School 127
Wanganui, Greyhound Buses Limited 126
'Warbirds over Wanaka' 293, 294
Ward, Sir Joseph 316
Warkworth *45*
water tower 130
Wattie, James *154*
Wedderburn *288*
Wei-Ming, Chen 258
Wellington *171-188*
  Athletic Park *186, 187*
  Cable Car Museum 171
  Courtenay Place *184*
  Freyberg Pool *185*
  Lambton Quay *180, 181*
  Michael Fowler Centre *178*
  Ngauranga Gorge *171*
  Oriental Bay *177*
  Star Boating Club 179
  Te Aro salt-water baths *185*
  Te Papa *180*
  The Terrace *180*
  War Memorial *183*
  Wellington Rowing Club *179*
  Westpac Stadium *186, 187*
  Willis Street *182*
Wellington Provincial Government 123
Wellington and Manawatu Railway Company 170
Wellsford *45*
West Arm, 310
Westland Tai Poutini National Park 226
Westland (the West Coast) *205-228*
Westport *208, 209*
Whakapapa Chateau 113
Whakatane *94*
Whale Rider 99
whale-watching 230

whalers 94, 96, 134, 147, 230, 260, 267, 312, 316, 317
Whangamomona *138,139*
Whanganui National Park 129
Whangarei *42, 43*
Whangaroa *24*
wharves *28, 30, 33, 37, 46, 52, 57, 58, 70, 71, 90, 98, 102, 133, 153, 174, 176, 178, 179, 190-193, 218, 266*
whisky 311
White, Henry Eli 156
White Island 94
Whitianga *71*
Williams, Henry 28
Williams, T.B. 128
Williams, Yvette *278*
Wilmot, E.H. 310
Wilmot Pass *309, 310*
Wilson, Ross 133
wine *6, 7,* 147, 155, 167, 194, 196
Wingatui *280, 281*
Winton *312*
Winton, Thomas 312
women
  first bus conductor *15*
  first cabinet minister 237
  first governor-general 65
  first honours graduate 241
  first mayor 65
  first member of Parliament 237
  first Olympic gold medal 278
  first prime minister *252*
  first town clerk 312
  right to vote 237
Woodville *161*
World Heritage area 305, 309
world's steepest street *278*

Y

yachting 29, 42, *71, 190*
Yates, Elizabeth 65

Graham Stewart

Where James Cook first sighted New Zealand: the statue of James Cook at Gisborne near the mouth of the Turanganui River with Young Nicks Head (Te Kuri) in the distance.

First published 2009, reprinted 2009

GRANTHAM HOUSE PUBLISHING (established 1985)
6/9 Wilkinson Street
Wellington 6011
NEW ZEALAND

Copyright © Graham Stewart

ISBN   978 1 86934 109 1

A catalogue record for this book is available
from the National Library of New Zealand.

Edited by Lorraine Olphert
Design and concept by Graham Stewart,
Bookprint Consultants Limited, Wellington
Printed by Bookprint International Limited